COMING HOME

Potent Forces for Spiritual growth
1. Association with advanced
    Spiritual practitioner
2. Daily practice of Contemplation

The Library of Spiritual Classics republishes out-of-print nonfiction of the quest for human growth, the evolution of consciousness, and the transformation of the spirit. Some of these works are well known; others have been previously neglected.

Other books in this series include:

The Gurdjieff Work by Kathleen Riordan Speeth

COMING HOME

THE EXPERIENCE
OF ENLIGHTENMENT
IN SACRED TRADITIONS

LEX HIXON

Foreword by Ken Wilber

JEREMY P. TARCHER, INC.
Los Angeles

Copyright acknowledgments appear on page 215

Library of Congress Cataloging in Publication Data

Hixon, Lex.
    Coming home : the experience of enlightenment in sacred
traditions / Lex Hixon.
        p.   cm.
    Reprint, with new foreword. Originally published: 1st ed. Garden
City, N.Y. : Anchor Press/Doubleday, 1978.
    Bibliography:
    1. Spiritual life—Comparative studies.   I. Title.
BL624.H55   1989
291.4'2—dc19   88-28651
ISBN 0-87477-503-5   CIP

Jeremy P. Tarcher, Inc.
9110 Sunset Blvd.
Los Angeles, CA 90069

Distributed by St. Martin's Press, New York
Manufactured in the United States of America
10 9 8 7 6 5 4 3 2

CONTENTS

*In anne Bancroft's
20th Century mystics &
Sages*

FOREWORD

"Enlightenment is the awakening to our primal harmony or, in another mystical language, to our rootedness in the Divine."

Thus begins what is, in my opinion, the single best introductory book ever written on the world's great mystical traditions. As Lex Hixon himself makes quite clear, *Coming Home* is not an attempt at an academic survey or a textbook of the historical and doctrinal details of each of the great wisdom traditions. There are many excellent books that already serve this function (Huston Smith's *The Religions of Man*, for example). Nor is this book an attempt at a philosophical justification of the mystical or enlightened state (W. T. Stace's *Mysticism and Philosophy* accomplishes this brilliantly). Nor is it even a general anthology culled from the various traditions. Such anthologies—Aldous Huxley's *The Perennial Philosophy* is still the best—are important because they demonstrate that however different the various wisdom traditions might outwardly appear, they nevertheless inwardly share certain profound and cross-cultural insights into the nature of absolute Spirit or Godhead. And the supreme insight shared by all of the great traditions is simply this: absolute Spirit or Godhead is the ultimate source, essence, and identity of each and every individual being. Absolute Spirit is one's own True Nature or Original Face, which is the face of the cosmos as well. There is only God; and so these anthologies eloquently proclaim.

Important and extremely valuable as these approaches are, Lex Hixon's approach cuts at right angles to all of them, not replacing or displacing, but complementing them. He simply assumes the truth of divine Spirit as manifested in and through the various wisdom traditions, and then, instead of telling you all the historical details and doctrines of the various traditions, he invites you to release yourself into Spirit as it manifests itself through each of these traditions. Each chapter is thus devoted to a particular path, from Taoism to Krishnamurti, from Zen to Plotinus, from Vedanta to Sufism. While each essay gives enough historical background to orient the reader, the real purpose is to talk you into the contemplative awareness that is the mystical heart of each tradition but that is itself beyond all talk. The intent is to use thinking to tease us out of thinking, to dive to the very heart of the particular path, and to allow us to release ourselves into the openness and illumined nature of the very Divine itself. Lex Hixon is not primarily interested in doctrine, dogma, or ideas about Spirit, however relevant they all might be, but rather in the vulnerable, open, empty, illumined, and direct experience or realization of Spirit itself, standing free at the Heart, outshining the world, radiant to infinity. It is this timeless awareness that he wants us to glimpse.

Because Spirit manifests itself only in and as the world of form—of apparently separate things and apparently different events, of seeming separation and isolation and alienation—it is in this diverse world that we must begin our search for the One beyond the Many, our Primordial Ground. Therefore, we need a vehicle, a *yana*, to take us to the formless shore beyond, even if the final realization is only that no vehicle was necessary or even possible. It is for this purpose that the world's great mystical paths have come into existence. They are not beliefs, not theories, not ideas, not theologies, and not doctrines. Rather, they are vehicles; they are experiential *practices*. They are experiments to *perform* (and thus see "through form"). They are something to *do* and then *be*, not something to merely think and then believe. Ultimately, there are no mystical doctrines or beliefs whatsoever; there are only mystical experiences and insights, all springing directly and immediately from the flow of one's own primordial experiencing in this very moment, illuminating all that is, like sunlight on the clearest of crystal autumn days.

This is the genius of Lex Hixon's book. He does not dwell on the forms, doctrines, and details of the various traditions, essential as they most definitely are. Rather, he takes us gently but almost immediately to the unending *conclusion* of each and every path—the mood and experience of enlightenment itself. Using the terms and sometimes the actual practices of each of the particular vehicles that he is discussing, he invites us, in each chapter, to release all forms, concepts, names, and thoughts, and to tacitly acknowledge and actually *feel* that which is always prior to thought and sensation—namely, our own primordial experiencing or basic awareness, the presence and flow of Spirit itself.

This fundamental and universal consciousness you and all beings possess fully at every moment. It is your simple and bare awareness in this moment *before* you manipulate it, name it, judge it, or in any way fiddle with it. It is always the case prior to your attempts to grasp it. And therefore, ultimately, there is no path to this primary, basic, and ultimate consciousness. There is no way to walk to your own feet. Rather, the various traditions provide ways to exhaust the seeking mind, and the effort to grasp in time that which is eternal, to exhaust the attempts to grasp in space that which is infinite, and to exhaust the "great search" for Spirit so that Spirit itself may shine forth of its own accord. As Eckhart said, "God is closer to me than I am to myself." God or Spirit is simply your ultimate Self or Consciousness now lighting the words on this page—a Self (or no-self) that is one and undivided in all sentient beings.

This enlightened understanding and realization is what each of the world's great wisdom traditions attempts to transmit to those who would consent to perform the great experiment in their own souls. And it is the timeless conclusion of this mystical experiment that Lex Hixon presents throughout this book. In each chapter he takes us from surface thinking and the world of will and seeking and forms to a deeper or contemplative understanding, itself devoid of form, seeking, restriction, or knowing. In that openness, flashes of enlightened mind can shine forth, taking you so radically beyond yourself that you actually discover your True Self or Original Nature, which is as close as your present experiencing and your own basic awareness in this very moment. To abide as that Awareness in the simplicity and luminosity of the present, without will or effort, is to be ushered into a magical world you never left and, thus, to understand what it means to be "coming home," a homecoming that is said to lead from time to eternity and from death to immortality.

Coming Home is a simple, brilliant book. It explains and epitomizes the best of the world's great mystical traditions. By centering on the heart of enlightenment, it blazes the path of no-path. In the traditional Tibetan gesture of welcome, gratitude, and deep appreciation, I touch my forehead to that of my friend Lex Hixon—he who is "rooted in the Divine," as this book so eloquently testifies.

—KEN WILBER
Boulder, Colorado
December 1988

INTRODUCTION

Enlightenment is the awakening to our primal harmony or, in another mystical language, to our rootedness in the Divine. From Enlightenment radiate the insight, compassion, and power needed to resolve individual and collective human problems as they continue to arise endlessly. Enlightenment is not a magical transcendence of the human condition but the full flowering of humanity, disclosing unity and equilibrium at the heart of the love and suffering we call life. All existence is revealed to the Enlightened human being as a seamless whole, as Divine Life. Some taste of this Enlightenment which consciously touches the Ultimate is possible for each of us. It need not be deferred to any future existence in heaven or on earth. Enlightenment is the secret essence of our consciousness, and the gradual revelation of this essence is the process of spiritual growth in which everyone is involved.

These essays present several universes or languages of Spirit whose central theme is Enlightenment. Each is unique, yet all are rich with mutual correspondences because they reflect one primal awareness. The spiritual dimension of culture is not an array of dogmatic world views bristling with contradictions but a spectrum of contemplative practices, equivalent in essence, which lead toward experience rather than toward doctrinal assertion. *Coming Home* attempts to open various doors into this spiritual dimension.

Coming Home is not a systematic study of sacred traditions but evokes the actual texture of Enlightenment as a process that occurs mysteriously in all cultures. The approach is impressionistic, even lyrical. As a film is meant to be viewed without interruption, each essay is designed to be read at one sitting, drawing the reader into a complete world of experience as film does. The quality of theater is enhanced by reading the essays aloud among friends. This book is an attempt to embody what Hermann Hesse pictures in his novel *The Bead Game:* a contemplative game of multicultural chess, noncompetitive and symphonic, through which healing and revealing harmonies are created, not just intellectually but as tangible, communally shared experience, similar to music.

The language and thought of these essays are not simplified for some hypothetical *general reader* but will engage any reader interested in the spiritual dimension of culture. There are no scholarly technicalities. The writing will make demands on your attention but does not presuppose advanced study of religion or philosophy. Being primarily an attempt to kindle intellectual and spiritual vision rather than to explain, these essays could be characterized as meditations. They require sympathetic participation rather than detached reading.

Perhaps it will be helpful to review the cultural moments woven together here. Heidegger invokes the Western philosophical and Christian mystical traditions. He is one of the deepest contemporary Western contemplative thinkers who has no traditional religious commitment. Krishnamurti, who also remains unassociated with religious tradition, translates into modern language the spirit of ancient Asian contemplative practice. By contrast, Ramakrishna, who lived from 1836 to 1886, was fully immersed in Indian cultural and religious forms. Yet he possessed a rare universal vision which could take these forms beyond their own limits while safeguarding their original integrity. Ramakrishna's ecstatic participation in the Hindu, Christian, and Muslim spirituality to which he was exposed expresses the all-embracing Tantric Way. By further contrast, the Indian sage Ramana Maharshi, who died in 1951 and a meeting with whom inspired Somerset Maugham's *The Razor's Edge*, essentially bypasses all religious and cultural forms, Eastern and Western. Ramana may be the Einstein of planetary spirituality, transcending previous approaches to religion as the General Theory of Relativity transcended earlier, more parochial systems of physics.

Moving now from the contemporary to the ancient, we contemplate the Zen Ox-herding pictures, representations of ten phases in the process of Enlightenment which have enhanced the deeper understanding of Buddhist practitioners since the twelfth century. The essay is illustrated with a contemporary version of the Ox-herding pictures by the American artist Eugene Gregan. The essay on Plotinus attempts to show that this mystical Platonic philosopher from the early centuries of the Christian Era is perhaps the most profound metaphysician of the spiritual quest who has appeared at any time in any culture. The essay closes with an account of my own experience, through spiritual imagination, of the ascent to the One about which Plotinus eloquently speaks.

The following three essays are intimately connected, exploring sister universes of Spirit: Judaism, Christianity, and Islam. The essay on Jewish Hasidic soul masters enters directly into the sphere of holy ecstasy, which is impenetrable by any rational approach. The essay on the letters of Saint Paul stresses the kinship between Paul as a mystical rabbi and the Hasidic teachings explored earlier. Paul's ecstatic experience on the road to Damascus is the seed for the mystical approach to the Messiah developed by Christian tradition. We next turn to a personal letter written to me from Sri Lanka by a contemporary Islamic sage, Bawa Muhaiyaddeen, who embodies the Sufi Way. Then, from the perspective of the Confucian and Taoist traditions of ancient China, we examine the themes encountered thus far, seeking guidance in the traditional ritual manner from the oracle text of the *I Ching*. This revelatory interlude resembles conversation with an ancient Chinese sage. Finally, the tenth essay attempts to gather and fuse all these languages and images into a contemplative experiment to be carried out by each reader. The Absolute of Advaita Vedanta, termed *Turiya* in Sanskrit, is related in this essay to contemplative practice in terms of a vivid experience which occurred to me during meditation.

Thus *Coming Home* culminates, not on the level of intellectual inquiry but in the sphere of spiritual practice and experience.

The story of my own path to the Spirit centers around an elderly Sioux spiritual leader, holy shaman in the role of Episcopal priest, who introduced me to prayer and meditation when I was nineteen. Father Deloria awakened in me a thirst for contemplative practice and mystical experience with stories of his grandfather, Tipisapa or Black Tipi, a traditional Lakota holy man. Through the medium of Christian spirituality, Vine Deloria practiced the long waiting in silence and experienced the sacred visions characteristic of Native American spirituality. He actually perceived a globe of intensely beautiful Divine Radiance, the presence of Wakantanka, the Great Spirit, floating at the foot of the Cross as he celebrated Communion. Thus my own spiritual life sprang up through the interplay of sacred traditions.

When I was twenty-four, I made acquaintance in New York City with Swami Nikhilananda, a senior monk of the Ramakrishna Order, urbane, scholarly, and far advanced in contemplative life. My wife and I were blessed to study and meditate with Nikhilananda in close relationship for the last eight years of his life. He was a direct disciple of Sarada Devi, wife of Ramakrishna, who is among the most radiant woman saints of modern times. In her immediate lineage I received initiation and spiritual training. Since then I have been further blessed by initiation and instruction from spiritual guides representing various traditions, deepening my appreciation for the all-embracing attitude expressed by Ramakrishna and others who share the universal vision.

Exploring this universal way while completing my doctorate in religion at Columbia University, I have produced weekly radio documentaries over the Pacifica station in New York City, interviewing well-known spiritual teachers from around the world and their close disciples. This experience has been rich but difficult to assimilate. The crosscurrents of spiritual practices and commitments immigrating to America and emerging from contemporary American culture are complex and confusing. *Coming Home* represents my own affirmation of the spiritual harmony that resolves this confusion. The resolution is not facile but has been long sought and pondered. Nor is it a position of naïve acceptance of various religious claims. Spiritual longing should be accompanied by sympathetic yet critical intelligence that continually reorients us to the most compassionate ethical values and the most comprehensive practice of contemplation.

Writing this book has involved an intense process of sharing with you, the reader, as the original talks on which the essays are based involved an intimate sharing with some twenty people of various ages and persuasions who attended my evening lectures at the New School for Social Research, in New York City, during the spring of 1975. Shared understanding moves deeper than private understanding, creating through words a kinship beyond words.

To the ancient saints and contemporary men and women of the Spirit too numerous to name who are my teachers, and to family, friends, and now readers, with whom I share the spiritual adventure, I offer gratitude. Perhaps human relationship is the most holy sacrament.

—LEX HIXON
New York City
May 1978

NOTE ON
TERMINOLOGY

The essays contain a variety of terms for Enlightenment and
what it reveals. These expressions belong to the same family
of meaning and yet carry subtle differences in connotation.
The term *primal awareness*, for instance, is used to evoke the
intrinsic or essential nature of human awareness, without
linking it to any particular sacred tradition. *Ultimate Consciousness* is used similarly to evoke the ground or source of
all phenomena. However, primal awareness and Ultimate
Consciousness, to which we awaken through the process of
Enlightenment, are not separate.

*True Nature, Original Mind, Turiya, Tao, Godhead, Allah, Di-
vine Mother, Messiah Nature, Christ Nature*—these and similar
expressions evoke one mystery in several keys. Their various
usages should not be regarded as contradictory, nor should
some be considered more adequate than others. Similarly,
expressions such as the *process of Enlightenment, awakening as
the One, God-realization, self-knowledge, kensho, Gnosis, illumination, coming home*, and *holy ecstasy* are members of a single
family of meaning, as are *sage, guru, tzaddik, saint, shaman*.
Yet these terms reflect the rich contrasts among various spiritual and cultural moods. There exists what we have called
primal harmony among these countless sacred languages and
images, but it cannot be described in systematic form.

I wish to thank my editor, Angela Iadavaia-Cox, who suggested this note and whose clarifying attention has been
brought to bear on every sentence of these essays. Again

and again she has heightened my awareness of you, the reader, allowing me to realize that the reader is a full partner in the subtle communication that is undertaken by any book about spiritual experience.

COMING HOME

CHAPTER ONE

CONTEMPLATIVE THINKING

The European and Asian Approaches of Heidegger and Krishnamurti

1895 - 1986

Imagine you are wandering through a vast cathedral. Countless stained-glass windows, radiant in the darkness, represent the modes of worship and ways of understanding that humanity has evolved throughout its history. Some windows picture Divine Presence through personal forms or attributes, and seekers worship before these windows with devotion. Other seekers, preferring the way of wisdom, contemplate stained-glass windows that present nothing personal, simply esoteric patterns evoking primal harmony and unity. Devotion and wisdom are alternate ways to Enlightenment. Some sacred traditions interweave both ways.

What occurs as we contemplate these cathedral windows? We are really experiencing Light, diffused through complicated contexts that have been created, individually and communally, by visionary artisans. And we cannot step outside this cathedral, which is human thinking, because we must depend on some personal and cultural medium. We cannot articulate any experience, even to ourselves, without some process of thinking. This is not imprisonment but simply the nature of the Light or Reality, which expresses itself as experience only through some particular medium.

1

We may feel disappointed. Can we never encounter directly whatever is *out there*, beyond the opaque windows of personal and cultural interpretation? Can we experience Reality only indirectly? What and where is the Source of this Light? Such inquiry leads us deeper into contemplative thinking, and as our contemplation intensifies, a surprising reversal of perspective occurs. This is the experience of Enlightenment, through which we cease to imagine ourselves simply *within* this cathedral of the human mind. We become aware that the essence of our consciousness is the essence of the Light that illuminates the countless windows. We realize Consciousness to be the Light which constitutes all phenomena. We are always shining *outside* the cathedral, but there is nothing *out there* to see, only to be. Our True Nature alone is there: Divine Radiance, or Ultimate Consciousness. Particular experiences can occur only through particular windows, but we *are* the Clear Light that the human mind, which has created this vast cathedral, refracts through all its languages and images.

Each window of devotion or wisdom translates the same radiance of Ultimate Consciousness by means of personal figures or symbolic patterns unique to itself. Through dedicated contemplation of even a single window, we can attune to Light, or Reality, and eventually realize that our intrinsic nature *is* this Light. Once realizing the universal cathedral to be flooded with the conscious Light of our True Nature, once Enlightenment has dawned, we are at home everywhere. We have been freed from the competition between worldviews, by understanding the essential equality of all windows of contemplation and the harmony between the ways of wisdom and of devotion. Everywhere in this vast cathedral, through all possible languages and images, we now recognize the Light, or Consciousness, which we *are*, which all beings *are*, which Being *is*.

This image of the cathedral illustrates the nature of contemplative thinking, a process natural to the mind by which thinking is led to its own core, or ground. Because contemplative thinking is not external to the ordinary functioning of the mind, it can be experienced without entering any special state of trance or ecstasy. Nor does such deep thinking depend on formal training. Even during ordinary thinking, the harmonizing and unifying flow of contemplation is always present. Each of us has immediate access to the contemplative mood the moment we explore the ground of our own awareness. Yet our access to deep thinking can be obscured by unfamiliarity. The natural contemplative mood often remains dormant until kindled by the touch of an awakened person.

Contemplative thinking is not confined to certain fields such as religion, art, or philosophy but flourishes subtly throughout every culture, often obscurely among small circles or secretly within the inner life of individuals who may not be aware of any mystical tradition. This ever-deepening way of contemplation, which follows devotion and wisdom to their Source, is perhaps the most precious human possibility. The holy person, or shaman, in every culture—poet musician, saint, warrior—is revered for the powerful touch that awakens and sustains deep thinking and its sense of discovery, freedom, and harmony. The figure of the shaman is a sacrament through which all members of the culture without exception can enter the mood of contemplation.

We present here two such individuals from the contemporary world. Heidegger, the German philosopher, emerges from Greek philosophical and Christian mystical traditions. Krishnamurti, the Indian sage, expresses an incisive Asian approach. Although from contrasting cultural environments, the contemplative thinking of both have a similar resonance. Both thinkers create stained-glass windows of wisdom rather than devotion. Their refusal to identify with any conventional religious context helps us to begin this study of contemplative life relatively free from our presuppositions about religious imagery. Yet Heidegger's experience of *Being* and Krishnamurti's experience of *Truth* constitute the fulfillment of the sacred quest in whatever cultural forms this quest is clothed.

Heidegger describes the most dangerous quality of our secular age as the obsession with the surface of thinking that distracts us from deep thinking. Heidegger terms this surface *calculative thinking*, not disparaging its ability to organize our world but warning against its power to absorb completely our energy and attention. Calculative thinking is not merely a euphemism for the approach of empirical science but characterizes any thinking process that plans to dominate and manipulate situations. Religious and artistic thinking at their surface are also calculative. Yet even the impoverishment of thinking when confined to its own surface cannot rob human consciousness of its essentially contemplative nature. As Heidegger affirms: *We can grow thought-poor or even thought-less only because man, at the core of his being, has the capacity to think . . . is destined to think . . . is a thinking, that is, a meditating being.*

Rather than organizing energy, deep thinking, suggests Heidegger, *contemplates the meaning which reigns in everything that is.* The contemplative mood is healing, stilling, strengthening. It opens one to the primal subject of all contemplation, which Heidegger terms *Being*, the radiance, or *meaning*, of which *reigns* everywhere. Deep thinking does not exclude surface thinking but allows the surface to become transparent to its ultimate ground, or Being. The botanist who is developing new strains of wheat need not renounce his scientific calculations when he awakens to deep thinking and contemplates the pervasive radiance of Being.

Although contemplative thinking is not beyond the reach of any person, practice is required, just as for the mastery of calculative thinking. Remarks Heidegger: *Meditative thinking does not just happen by itself any more than does calculative thinking. At times it requires a greater effort. It demands more practice. It is in need of even more delicate care than any other genuine craft.* We must develop the art of waiting, releasing our hold and trusting in a spiritual process that is natural and spontaneous. As Heidegger suggests, deep thinking *must be able to bide its time to await as does the farmer whether the seed will come up and ripen.*

Stressing the simplicity, earthiness, and immediate accessibility of deep thinking, Heidegger continues: *Meditative thinking need by no means be high-flown. It is enough if we dwell on what lies close and meditate on what is closest. . . . here and now, here, on this patch of home ground.* The home ground that is closest is primal awareness as it pervades our daily activity. In the present age of technology, we cannot become a planet of rural villagers, yet the natural simplicity and harmony of village life is available, wherever we find ourselves, through contemplative thinking. Contemplation is our spiritual rootedness.

When divorced from contemplative thinking, calculative thinking, with all its apparent practicality, becomes an abstraction. It develops technologies that possess manipulative powers and offer an illusory sense of tangibility but cannot nourish humanity. Calculative thinking can never genuinely alleviate human problems unless it is integrated with deep thinking. Thinking confined to its own surface begins to live only for organizing, manipulating, dominating. Such thinking obscures our intrinsic harmony. Yet the fact that we often notice a peaceful strength in those who have mastered some aspect of calculative thinking—musician, mechanic, potter, mathematician—indicates that there are not two separate dimensions of thinking, contemplative and calculative, but a single flow of awareness. The separation is a symptom of spiritual disharmony to which human beings have always been subject, but perhaps more intensely so in this secular and technological age. The healing of this disharmony between calculation and contemplation is the process of Enlightenment, which discloses the essence of all thinking to be contemplation. This process is not just for a few saints or yogis but for everyone.

Deep thinking emerges organically from our own patch of

ground, our own garden, from simple seeds. It is never abstract but remains intensely practical because it is a personal practice, a way of self-reliance, such as growing our own vegetables. Yet its promising nature is obscured by its very simplicity. As Heidegger suggests: *Perhaps the answer we are looking for lies at hand; so near that we all too easily overlook it. For the way to what is near is always the longest and thus the hardest for us humans. This is the way of meditative thinking.* During our pilgrimage through the cathedral, the Light that illuminates the stained-glass windows of contemplation is eventually realized to be our own Light. This is what is near: primal awareness. Yet the process of coming home into this nearness is subtle and demanding.

As we begin to read from Heidegger's *Conversation on a Country Path About Thinking,* a dramatic interchange between three contemplative thinkers, we may find the language difficult to follow. Heidegger creates new words and new ways of formulating thoughts which may appear convoluted but are actually courageous attempts to see more simply and directly. This condensed dialogue is an illustration of the nature of contemplative thinking, a transforming walk along a country path to the primal awareness at the ground of Being.

Beginning with a basic paradox of the mystical path, expressed by the Zen archer who looks away from the target while releasing the arrow, one of Heidegger's characters remarks about the approach to contemplation: *the nature of thinking can be seen only by looking away from thinking.* Thus we must turn from our impulse to calculate, looking away into the sky or across the hills of our being, in order to become receptive to the deep nature of thinking beneath its surface function as willing. As the second participant in the dialogue responds: *In answer to your question as to what I really wanted from our meditation on the nature of thinking . . . I want non-willing.* This non-willing comes into play as we look away from the target. One cannot willfully grasp non-willing but must be released into it. As the third participant in this conversation remarks, *You want a non-willing in the sense of a renouncing of willing, so that through this we may release . . . ourselves to the sought-for essence of a thinking that is not a willing.* The contemplative thinker does not *grasp the essence of thinking* but is, rather, *released to the essence of thinking.* This distinction is not simply wordplay. If we expect to grasp a particular meaning, forcibly extracting the essence of the subject, then we remain on the level of calculative thinking. Even the use of ordinary syntax, a verb and its object, such as *I know the essence of thinking*, represents a subtle involvement with the mode of willful control. Contemplative thinking, by contrast, is perfect release, which is, fundamentally, release from willing. The contemplative no longer asserts, *I know the essence*, but reflects, *I do not will to know, but await the essence in perpetual not-knowing.* Significant cultural and scientific advances have developed from the ambitious willing of human beings to grasp essences and thus control energy, but it will never release us to the nature of contemplation.

The three-way conversation continues, each thinker responding to the other like instruments in a musical composition.

—*If only I possessed already the right releasement, then I would soon be freed of that task of weaning from the will.*

—*So far as we can wean ourselves from willing, we contribute to the awakening of releasement.*

—*Say, rather, to keeping awake for releasement.*

To regard our personal efforts as contributing to the awakening of releasement is to become involved in subtle calculation. The phrase *keeping awake for releasement* expresses more accurately this dawning of the contemplative mood. We must realize that we *already possess the right releasement,* because the task of weaning from will is interpenetrated by willing itself. Willing can never transcend the will. The only way to be free from willing is to experience the truth that perfect releasement already exists. As the conversation continues:

—*On our own we do not awaken releasement in ourselves.*

—*Thus releasement is affected from somewhere else.*

—Not affected, but let in. Releasement awakens when our nature is let in so as to have dealings with that which is not a willing.
Continual care is shown by Heidegger to reorient from the active to the passive voice, from the willful sense of *affecting releasement* to the contemplative sense of being *let in*. But this partiality of deep thinking to the passive mood in the realm of language does not mean passivity in the realm of action. This is made clear by the further conversation of the three friends as they stroll aimlessly along the country path:

—You speak of a letting-be and give the impression that what is meant is a kind of passivity. . . . I think I understand that it is in no way a matter of weakly allowing things to slide and drift along.

—Perhaps a higher acting is concealed in releasement than is found in all the actions within the world.

—Which higher acting is yet no activity.

Although emerging directly from Western philosophical tradition, Heidegger's deep thinking evokes the egoless action of Zen and Taoist contemplatives, whose perfect relaxation in the midst of action *lets in* the flow of the Tao, or nonwilling, *lets it be* in a way that allows for stillness at the center of intense activity. This is what Heidegger terms *releasement*.

One of the three friends inquires, *What has releasement to do with thinking?*, and another responds, *Nothing, if we conceive thinking in the traditional way as re-presenting*. This is the paradox with which we began: the essence of thinking has literally nothing *to do* with calculative or representational thinking, for deep thinking is not *doing* but *being*. Calculative thought is re-presented, habitually reconstructed from the memory banks of convention, both personal and cultural. By contrast, contemplation, or the essence of thinking, is simply presence. Representational thinking catalogues useful patterns of thought and displays them again and again in order to organize energy. Non-representational, or contemplative, thinking awakens a sense of our intrinsic releasement from all patterns of organization, which are indispensable at the surface of thinking but absent in its depths.

We may wonder at this point how to recognize and to

practice contemplative thinking, since it camot be pictured
or represented. The dialogue moves in this same direction.

—*With the best of will I can't re-present to myself this nature
of thinking.*

—*Precisely because this will of yours, and your mode of thinking
as re-presenting, prevent it.*

—*Then, what in the world am I to do?*

—*We are to do nothing but wait.*

Genuine meditative waiting is discovered only through the
breakdown of willing which begins with the mood expressed
in the dialogue as *what in the world am I to do?* This mood can
be one of despair or dispassion, renunciation or ecstasy, but
the move from willful thinking to meditative waiting requires
an authentic revolution in our habitual patterns of awareness.
Deep thinking neither entails *doing* nor does it occur *in the
world,* for the *world* and *doing* are aspects of calculative thinking. Therefore contemplation does not provide any direct
answer to the puzzle *what in the world am I to do?* Contemplation can never be a process of satisfying the will.

The proper environment for the practice of meditative waiting is what Heidegger terms *openness* and describes through
the following visual metaphor: *The field of vision is something
open, but its openness is not due to our looking.* Openness is not
due to any specific point of view but is, rather, the absence
of single-perspective perceiving and thinking. And openness, not created by any effort on our part, is always present
as primal awareness. Upon this openness we superimpose
various worlds which are, in Heidegger's words, *but the side
facing us of an openness which surrounds us, an openness which
is filled with the appearances of what, to our representing, are
objects.* These facing sides of openness are the worlds that
we organize through surface thinking. To representational
thinking our world appears to contain objects, but it is revealed to contemplation as the open expanse of primal awareness. Mystics often assert, in their various languages, that
there are no objects, that all is one flow, that what we actually
perceive are the facets or textures of one harmonious Reality.

Heidegger's dramatic characters now begin to explore this Reality, which reveals itself through openness.

—It strikes me as something like a region, an enchanted region where everything belonging there returns to that in which it rests.

—Strictly speaking, a region for everything is not one region among many, but the region of all regions.

—The enchantment of this region might well be . . . its regioning. The noun *region* may be taken to mean a definable space and thereby become the subject of calculative thinking. The verbal form *regioning* suggests the incalculable quality of openness, its *enchantment*. This continual erasing of subtle calculations as they arise is contemplative thinking. Although there is a dimension of contemplation in which even this activity of the mind is stilled, significant thinking can be done *about* contemplation *through* contemplation itself. This is the process Heidegger is engaged in here: guiding others toward the core of thinking and providing them with some sense of the carefulness and alertness that are required to sustain contemplative thinking.

Heidegger uses the voices of this dialogue to describe his own mystical experience of being drawn from our organized world into the trackless and radiant core of Being. The power of his words is perhaps better appreciated by reading them aloud. They describe *regioning* as the primordial gift offered to human beings: refuge in the sacred heart of Being. *The region gathers, just as if nothing were happening, each to each and each to all into an abiding, while resting in itself. Regioning is a gathering and resheltering for an expanded resting in an abiding. . . . That-which-regions is an abiding expanse which, gathering all, opens itself, so that in it openness is halted and held, letting everything merge in its own resting.* Each of these phrases echoes expressions in traditional mystical literatures that describe ecstatic experiences of leaving objects behind as one is caught up into the Divine or as one expands into the Absolute.

Carlos Castaneda, a contemporary anthropologist, was led by his Yaqui Indian guide, the sorcerer Don Juan, into just

such an *enchanted regioning*. Whenever pushed or tricked outside the boundaries of calculative thinking by his shamanistic
teacher, Castaneda would enter a dimension of consciousness in which objects disappeared, or appeared bizarrely in
refutation of their own objectivity. As Heidegger remarks,
*Things which appear in that-which-regions no longer have the char-
acter of objects.* This is not to deny the coherent existence of
objects within our various organized worlds. It would be
foolish to refuse to consider a watch, for instance, as an
instrument by which we can tell time. However, were we
fully aware of being released into *that-which-regions*, a watch
would no longer appear as a separate object but as a facing
side of openness, useful yet utterly transparent as it returns
and abides in the expanse of Being.

But what does this actually mean? One of the three participants shares a frustration we may feel ourselves.

—*I must confess that I can't quite re-present in my mind all that
you say about region, expanse, and abiding, and about return and
resting.*

—*Probably it can't be re-presented at all.*

If we attempt to develop, as we read, a clear picture of *that-
which-regions* and its relation to our conventional, objective
world, then we are falling away from contemplative thinking.
It requires strength to stay with deep thinking, not the strength
of will power but the strength of resting, opening, waiting.
Our tendency is to surge back into calculative activity, to
begin representing again, vaguely or precisely. Heidegger's
language attempts to defy this representational urge, while
remaining engaged in authentic naming. Without actually
describing, he allows various names of Being to be revealed
in a non-representational way. As the three participants in
the dialogue reflect:

—*Any description would reify it.*

—*Nevertheless, it lets itself be named and, being named, it can
be thought about.*

—*Only if thinking is no longer re-presenting.*

But how are we actually to engage in this process of contemplative thinking? Are we to be kept waiting perpetually for an answer to the simple question of how to begin? Heidegger responds in the affirmative by suggesting that the contemplative mood is simply one of waiting: *Perhaps we are now close to being released into the nature of thinking . . . through waiting for its nature. . . . Waiting lets re-presenting entirely alone. It really has no object.* Contemplation is waiting without prospect, waiting for waiting's sake. This waiting is the access to deep thinking, which does not obliterate surface thinking— simply lets it alone. However, we cannot assert, *I am waiting for contemplative thinking to begin,* because that is calculative thinking: waiting-for rather than pure waiting. Deep thinking never begins, because it is always there, pulsing at the core of all thought—waiting. Through this waiting, a subtle transformation of ordinary consciousness occurs and distance becomes nearness, waiting becomes abiding. In Heidegger's words, *Waiting releases itself into openness . . . into the expansive distance . . . in whose nearness it finds the abiding in which it remains.*

At this point the participants in the dialogue unexpectedly come upon a non-representational definition of the essence of thinking. This definition is suggested by the transformation of consciousness in which distance becomes nearness.

—*Then, thinking would be coming-into-the-nearness of distance.*

—*That is a daring definition of its nature which we have chanced upon.*

—*I only brought together that which we have named, but without representing anything to myself.*

As the non-representational artist brings together creative movements that have no pictorial reference, so must we express *that-which-regions* with pure gestures of contemplative thinking that have no reference to the organized world of will. We are not to build any system of assertions but simply keep our balance in deep thinking, which flows like a river rather than becoming an abstract structure. Representational thought naturally attempts to crystallize the flow of awareness into reliable structures. To transcend this instinctive urge to represent, we must, in Heidegger's terms, *open as openness*, a flowering or melting no less natural to the human being than the crystallizing or organizing process.

When Heidegger speaks of the *opening of openness*, this is not meant as a Zen Buddhist puzzle, or *koan*, which generates heat to evaporate thinking. The Zen attitude toward thinking often involves distrust or even disdain. Heidegger, by contrast, moves deeper by means of thought, accepting and even revering the thinking process, allowing it to refine itself gradually in order to become a mode of revelation. Heidegger thus reflects the reverence for thinking inherent in the Greek philosophical tradition. For Zen, Enlightenment is revealed through rigorous un-naming, whereas the process of revelatory naming leads to Plato's vision of the Good. But Heidegger, no less than the Zen Master, recognizes the mystery of this contemplative process, whether it is understood as naming or un-naming. Remarks one of the three participants: *Perhaps these names are not the result of designation. They are owed to a naming in which the name and the named occur together.* If we imagine that it is we who are conferring names, or designating objects, then we are engaged in the activity of willing or representing. However, if we recognize that the name and the named occur together spontaneously, then we are not willing the process of naming into existence but releasing ourselves to contemplative naming, as it already exists.

Heidegger's mystical naming is closer to the traditional practice of chanting the Divine Name than to the organizing and controlling function which the naming process usually serves. Islamic mystics, for instance, spend hours repeating the Divine Name Allah, which has the power to awaken contemplation spontaneously as a flower blossoms from its seed. Heidegger releases this same holy power of the Name, but in a philosophical rather than devotional mood. Through this contemplative naming—*the opening of openness, that-which-regions, the expanse of Being*—one who becomes attuned experiences a power that operates through philosophical intuition as the word *Allah* operates through religious devotion.

At this level of contemplation, Heidegger ceases to be an individual thinker with his own personal limits and becomes a focus for the transmission of the Western mystical tradition, which is still alive in our secular twentieth century.

As the devotional chanting of the Divine Name, so Heidegger's philosophical chanting is not a process directed toward an end—both are modes of eternal waiting in Divine Presence or simply Presence. In Heidegger's words, *Waiting is . . . the relation to that-which-regions, insofar as waiting releases itself to that-which-regions, and in doing so lets that-which-regions reign purely as such.* Waiting is the way and the goal: a waiting that never ends, a perpetual inbreath. Any other relationship, such as *finding,* would stimulate the sense of possessing that reifies or objectifies what is *found.* Enlightenment or releasement into *that-which-regions,* can never be *found,* for it has never been lost. Simply as conscious beings, we are already encompassed by *that-which-regions,* or primal awareness. We remain unillumined insofar as we have not yet released ourselves into *that-which-regions,* insofar as we have not learned to wait in openness, neither representing nor willing.

Because it abides beyond the domain of will, releasement or Enlightenment, although always the essence of thinking, is experienced as a gift. As Heidegger remarks: *Authentic releasement must be based upon that-which-regions, and must have received from it the movement toward it.* This is the echo, in Heidegger's contemplative thinking, of the traditional theistic sense of Divine Grace by which the devotee *receives from God the movement toward God.* In the nontheistic mood, such as expressed by Zen Buddhism, there is no God who showers Grace, yet Enlightenment dawns in the same graceful manner, free from any sense of personal striving, deserving, or attaining. Divine Grace and spontaneous awakening describe the same process of receptivity and gratitude in two different languages, the process Heidegger terms *receiving the movement toward that-which-regions from that-which-regions itself.* Whether speaking theistic or nontheistic language, those who have experienced illumination intimate a thankful sense of *being lifted up* or *letting go*. In both these modes of mystical experience, gratitude arises spontaneously as when we receive a loving gift.

The gift of Enlightenment is recognized as a return to our Divine Source or to our True Nature. As Heidegger suggests: *He is released to it in his being, insofar as he originally belongs to it . . . Waiting upon something is based on our belonging in that upon which we wait.* Enlightenment already is, because we belong there, we are at home there, and therefore it does not need actively to be brought about. However, the paradox remains that much struggle, both anguished and joyful, is required to open out of the active, willing, calculative dimension into the perpetual waiting of releasement or Enlightenment. Yet this waiting, which is both the practice of contemplation and its goal, is not frustrating or incomplete, because we already belong there—waiting. This sense of belonging to the contemplative mood is the secret essence of all thinking. As the Zen master proclaims, there is not the slightest difference between our ordinary mind and the mind of Buddha. There is no intrinsic separation between the surface of thinking and its depths.

Heidegger evokes Enlightenment entirely in terms of Western tradition. His understanding is more profound than many contemplatives, Eastern or Western, because he envisions releasement or Enlightenment as perpetual waiting rather than as the attainment of a particular state or definable goal. As one participant in the dialogue remarks, far along the country path of contemplation: *Releasement is indeed the release of oneself from . . . representation and so a relinquishing of willing . . . exulting in waiting, through which we become more waitful and more void.*

Voidness is a term often used in Mahayana Buddhism to express the nature of Reality. Heidegger's parallel term is *openness*. Perpetual waiting as voidness or openness, which is Enlightenment, paradoxically generates intense feelings of gratitude. For worshipers of the personal God, this thankfulness flows toward the Divine. For those who meditate in the mood of impersonal wisdom, there is thankfulness simply for its own sake. Thus the participants in this dialogue eventually come to recognize contemplative thinking as *thanking*, in Heidegger's words, *that thanking which does not have to thank for something but only thanks for being allowed to thank*. Elsewhere Heidegger writes simply *denken ist danken*, to think is to thank. This ultimate *thanking*, which has been revealed as the essence of thinking, is the all-embracing sense of nearness, in Heidegger's words, *moving-into-nearness . . . in the sense of letting-oneself-into-nearness*. This nearness, which is distance transmuted by contemplation, is the intimate sense that we ourselves are the Light illuminating the stained-glass windows of all personal and cultural contexts. The Light or Consciousness which we are is ultimately near. It is *nearness*.

At the culmination of Heidegger's dialogue, the sacred and mysterious nature of *nearness* is revealed as a feminine principle of intoxicating and transforming power. The participants are released into a lyrical mood in which they worshipfully contemplate this feminine Wisdom at the core of their own thinking. The country path has disappeared into the pathless meadow of primal awareness, where the three friends blend their voices to praise contemplative thinking herself.

—*She binds together without seam or edge or thread . . .*
—*She neighbors, because she works only with nearness . . .*
—*If she ever works, rather than rests . . .*
—*While wandering upon the depths of the height . . .*
—*Then, wonder can open what is locked? . . .*
—*By way of waiting . . .*
—*If this is released . . .*
—*And human nature remains appropriated to that . . .*
—*Whence we are called . . .*

Heidegger's dialogue leads us almost imperceptibly into contemplation, neither presenting the anguish and ecstasy of this revolution in consciousness nor revealing how the ordinary world appears after this revolution has deepened into Enlightenment. We therefore turn to Krishnamurti, whose Asian approach to contemplative thinking is more practical and experiential, remaining silent concerning the philosophical themes on which Heidegger dwells. Neither approach is superior to the other. Heidegger, because of his background in academic philosophy, sets himself the task of melting the crystallized structures of the Western philosophical tradition, which, he ardently insists, has become centered in calculative thinking and divorced from its essence, which is contemplation. Krishnamurti, by contrast, developed his approach in the Indian ambiance of ambitious spiritual practice, and thus chooses to expose the calculative thinking that masquerades as various forms of mystical quest.

Krishnamurti suggests that the very structure of quest, which projects its own fulfillment into some more or less distant time or state of consciousness, further binds human nature, rather than, in Heidegger's terms, releasing us to our intrinsic releasement. Just as rational investigation is recognized by Heidegger to be calculative rather than contemplative, so religious search is perceived by Krishnamurti as a function of what the mind willfully projects rather than as an access to what he calls *Truth*. Neither rational nor religious explanations open directly into contemplation. Such explanations even serve to obscure the core, or ground, of thinking. However, there is never any actual separation from deep thinking, for the essence of awareness is already contemplation, fully abiding as the expanse that Heidegger terms *Being* and Krishnamurti *Truth*.

Krishnamurti's approach, like that of Heidegger, begins from a consideration of the basic nature of thinking, finding its essence to be empty, or open. Krishnamurti questions: *Does thinking begin with a conclusion? Is thinking a movement from one conclusion to another? Can there be thinking if thinking is positive? Is not the highest form of thinking negative?* Krishnamurti's *negative thinking*, similar to what Heidegger terms *meditative thinking*, dives beneath the surface of conclusions or calculations. Surface thinking is what Krishnamurti calls *knowledge*, asking: *Is not all knowledge an accumulation of definitions, conclusions, and positive assertions?* Once again, there is no disparagement here of ordinary knowledge, or the surface of thinking, simply the warning that the surface should not be allowed to obscure the depths. Remarks Krishnamurti: *Knowledge is only a part of life, not the totality, and when that part assumes all-consuming importance, as it is threatening to do now, then life becomes superficial.* The central danger for this technological and secular age is the knowledge or calculative thinking that draws more and more of our energy and attention by making promises it cannot keep. Observes Krishnamurti: *More knowledge, however wide and cunningly put together, will not resolve our human problems; to assume that it will is to invite frustration and misery. Something much more profound is needed.* What is needed is to open into the core of our own thinking process.

Krishnamurti's *negative thinking* can be seen in his dialogue with seekers engaged in various forms of positive thinking. These seekers are filled with the assumptions and the imagery of their particular search, and Krishnamurti attempts to empty or to open them. One such seeker of knowledge who had lived in monasteries around the world exploring esoteric traditions remarked to Krishnamurti: *I am not sure I understand you . . . when you say that knowledge must be set aside to understand truth.* This highly dedicated seeker explained thus his own presupposition: *Given a first-rate mind and a capacity to accumulate knowledge, a man should be able to do immense good. . . . I am consumed with this urge to know.* The more intense our motivation the more completely we can become confined in the endlessly self-perpetuating pattern of quest. Since our primal awareness is already Truth, the attitude of quest is inappropriate. To this perpetual seeker, Krishnamurti remarks: *Positive thinking is the process of conformity, and the mind that conforms can never be in a state of discovery. . . . Truth must be discovered anew from moment to moment, it is not an experience that can be repeated . . . it is a timeless state . . .*

not a state to be achieved or a point towards which the mind can evolve or grow. This awakening into the timeless is without effort and instantaneous, because it already exists. Yet what Heidegger terms *willing* is so strong in this seeker that he immediately conceives the transition to primal awareness as an arduous act of will power, a thorough renunciation: *I think I understand what you mean, but is it not immensely difficult to renounce all that one has gathered?* Such renunciation would be calculative thinking. Krishnamurti simply replies: *To give up in order to gain is no renunciation at all.* The impulse to calculate, the will to accumulate—these surface functions of thinking must become transparent to the depths of thinking. Krishnamurti suggests no particular method or quest but recommends that awareness simply be aware of itself as intrinsically timeless, not bound to the network of definitions and assertions we call *time.* Timeless awareness is not static or blank but flows with life. Time is simply calculation, and timelessness the absence of calculation.

To illustrate the nature of timeless awareness, Krishnamurti relates his own perceptions in poetic passages that accompany his conversations. The sharp interchanges with seekers, through which Krishnamurti attempts to cut the umbilical cord of quest, present the drama of awakening to contemplative thinking. The transcriptions of his own timeless awareness, which are perhaps best appreciated as haiku in prose, reveal the nature of Enlightenment or primal awareness itself. Writes Krishnamurti: *It had rained all night and most of the morning and now the sun was going down behind dark, heavy clouds. There was no color in the sky, but the perfume of the rain-soaked earth filled the air. The frogs had croaked all night long with persistency and rhythm, but with the dawn they became silent.* Thus timeless awareness remains awake all night, raining as the rain, croaking as the frogs. This description presents directly what Heidegger suggests philosophically when he writes, *It is enough if we dwell on what lies close, and meditate on what is closest . . . here on this patch of home ground,* this home ground of rain awareness, frog awareness, silence awareness.

Krishnamurti's language is ordinary and clear, just as the nature of the primal awareness which is its source. He continues: *One of those large brown eagles was making wide circles in the sky, floating on the breeze without a beat of its wings. Hundreds of people on bicycles were going home after a long day at the office.* The eagle and the office workers, regardless of their various senses of limitation and need, express the same wide-circling, homecoming awareness. There is neither the mundane nor the sublime. *A large group had stopped, with their bicycles resting against their bodies, and were animatedly discussing some issue, while nearby a policeman wearily watched them.* There is precise psychological observation in timeless awareness. No level of perception is dulled. *The road was full of brown puddles, and the passing cars splashed one with dirty water which left dark marks on one's clothing.* All the apparent ugliness of the human world is perfectly visible, but there is no profound anger or frustration: our clothing is stained, not our conscious being. *A boy came along carrying on his head an old kerosene tin. . . . He had bright eyes and an extraordinarily cheerful face; he was thin but strongly built. . . . He wore a shirt and a loincloth, both the color of the earth.* Contemplative awareness is simple and youthful, dressed in earth colors, carrying the burden of time or calculation with poise and nonchalance. An alertness and unusual cheerfulness are its only visible characteristics.

As he contemplates the blessing of Truth, Krishnamurti's description of timeless awareness overflows into an ecstasy that remains simple and unadorned, quickly dissolving back into the ordinary flow of perception. *There was a blessing in the air, a love that covered everything, a gentleness that was simple, without calculation, a goodness that was ever flowering. Abruptly the boy stopped singing and turned towards a dilapidated hut that stood some distance back from the road.* This is what releasement into *that-which-regions* actually is: awareness itself, from which nothing is excluded. Social inequity, for instance, is quite visible in the dilapidated home to which the boy is returning. There is no obstruction or contradiction between various forms of responsible perception required at the surface of thinking and the contemplative repose at its depths. Nor does timeless awareness involve any sense of superiority or specialness. The young boy is not concerned with the blessing of Truth, but radiates that blessing through his alertness and cheerfulness. His homecoming is neither rich nor poor, simply aware.

Krishnamurti's first visitor, a seeker on the way of wisdom, was confronted by the fact that his intense desire to accumulate knowledge, even esoteric knowledge, had limited him to the surface of thinking. We should observe as well Krishnamurti's confrontation with a seeker on the way of devotion. The ripening process of this second visitor took some twenty-five years, he tells Krishnamurti, beginning with the phase of worldly success as a well-educated, happily married, securely employed government official. This level of social and personal attainment is not to be disdained as superficial. Until awakened to timeless awareness, all of us are driven by the same desire to discipline, to organize, to possess, and thereby to be fulfilled. Such longing, in its countless forms, is calculative thinking, and religious longing, as Krishnamurti's second visitor was finally to discover, is not necessarily more liberating than any form of longing. Longing provides an essential clue but must ultimately dissolve into its own source.

When this successful man decided, in traditional Indian fashion, to renounce family and career for a life devoted exclusively to meditative practice, his longing intensified but did not dissolve into Enlightenment. After years of study and rigorous discipline in meditation, this seeker became blessed by visions of Buddha, Christ, and Krishna. He remained for some time on this exhilarating plateau of spiritual experience until hearing a discourse by Krishnamurti, who stated: . . . *without self-knowledge, which in itself is meditation, all meditation is a process of self-hypnosis, a projection of one's own thought and desire.* The visitor courageously came to Krishnamurti and revealed the impact of these words: *I see that what you say is perfectly true, and it's a great shock to me to perceive that I have been caught in the images or projections of my own mind. I now realize very profoundly what my meditation has been. For twenty-five years I have been held in a beautiful garden of my own making; the personages, the visions were the outcome of my particular culture and of the things I have desired, studied and absorbed. I now understand the significance of what I have been doing, and I am more than appalled at having wasted so many precious years.*

Consider again the image of the cathedral through which we wander, experiencing various stained-glass windows and encountering through them the Light that Krishnamurti calls Truth. As long as we naïvely imagine that the colors or the figures in these windows are themselves the Source of Light, we have not awakened to what Krishnamurti terms *self-knowledge,* the understanding that our primal awareness itself is the Light that illuminates all personal and cultural contexts. Without this understanding, whatever visions and insights occur—artistic, religious, scientific, interpersonal—are mere accumulation rather than actual realization of our nature as timeless awareness. Krishnamurti expresses an intensely critical attitude toward wandering through this cathedral, naïvely seeking fulfillment from the patterns and images of the various windows. For Krishnamurti, dependence on esoteric systems or devotional imagery can and should be severed immediately by self-knowledge, by direct attention to awareness itself as intrinsically empty, open, timeless, complete.

Krishnamurti's visitor has plunged into the dramatic revolution that transmutes calculative thinking into contemplative thinking: *I can see that what I have come to in my meditation is a dead end, though only a few days ago it seemed so full of glorious significance. However much I would like to, I can't go back to all that self-delusion and self-stimulation. . . . You have no idea what I have been through during the last two days! The structure which I had so carefully and painfully built up over a period of twenty-five years has no meaning any more, and it seems to me that I shall have to start all over again.* Recognizing that his visitor is still subtly enchanted by calculative thinking, Krishnamurti replies: *May it not be that there is no restarting at all . . . ? If one were to start again, one might be caught in another illusion, perhaps in a different manner. What blinds us is the desire to achieve an end, a result: but if we perceive that the result we desire is still within the self-centered field, then there would be no thought of achievement.*

Krishnamurti explains to the distraught seeker: *You have practiced self-control, mastered thought, and concentrated on the furthering of experience. This is a self-centered occupation, it is not meditation: and to perceive that it is not meditation is the beginning of meditation.* Meditation, or contemplation, is a continual beginning over with the intuition that there is nothing to begin, free from the motivation to build any structure. If we engage in some process of articulation that we think of as contemplation, we will build a structure that must then be dismantled. Simply the intuition that primal awareness never builds or articulates is what Krishnamurti calls *the beginning of meditation.* He continues: *Freedom from the false does not come about through the desire to achieve it; it comes when the mind is no longer concerned with success, with the attainment of an end. There must be the cessation of all search, and only then is there a possibility of the coming into being of that which is nameless.*

Still under the spell of calculative thinking, the visitor replies: *All this involves time and patience, doesn't it?* This inveterate seeker is ready to begin a whole new project or projection, ready to sacrifice another twenty-five years to achieve the new goal he imagines Krishnamurti to be suggesting. Krishnamurti answers: *An ambitious man, worldly or otherwise, needs time to gain his end. Mind is the product of time . . . and thought working to force itself from time only strengthens its enslavement to time. Time exists only when there is a psychological gap between what is and what should be. . . . To be aware of the falseness of this whole manner of thinking is to be free from it—which does not demand any effort, any practice. Understanding is immediate, it is not of time.* This is the way of instantaneous Enlightenment. Yet Zen Buddhist practitioners engage in rigorous meditation usually for some five years before they experience the first *kensho,* or sudden Enlightenment. This is the ripening process. These earnest practitioners are meditating all that apparent time simply to dismantle the idea of time, to dissolve the calculation that they must strive for some goal called Enlightenment. As Heidegger suggests, releasement already exists. We already belong to *that-which-regions.* We have never strayed from our home ground. Coming into this nearness is the nature of thinking in its depth.

Don Juan is a magical sorcerer who transforms conventional objects in space and time in order to undercut the representational thinking of his student, Carlos Castaneda. Don Juan's sorcery makes use of visionary states of mind that call into question the objectivity of any mental state, leaving us no *world* with which to identify. Krishnamurti is a psychological sorcerer, who undercuts our world of calculation by exposing the psychological evasions we declare to be the search for Truth. The concept of search is the veil that obscures the timeless nature of awareness. Heidegger is a philosophical sorcerer, who, through the revelatory power of language, opens our surface thinking into the deep thinking which *is* the expanse of Being. The sorcery or shamanistic drama of these awakened individuals undercuts or transforms the *world* and *time.* The mode of expression developed by each is a stained-glass window through which we can contemplate the Light of primal awareness. Don Juan, Krishnamurti, and Heidegger have created radiant windows. We can stand, gaze, and be inspired. But eventually we must ourselves awaken into the nearness of primal awareness. We can then freely and reverently contemplate all cathedral windows, understanding our own essential nature to be the Clear Light they transmit.

CHAPTER TWO

THE TANTRIC WAY OF THE GODDESS KALI

HINDU

Ramakrishna of Bengal

1836 - 1886

Ramakrishna was completely at home in all the moods of spiritual expression he encountered, from Christianity and Islam to widely contrasting strands of Hinduism. Born in 1836 in a rural village of Bengal untouched by European influence, Ramakrishna expressed a universal spiritual vision rare in any culture. He experienced all religions as a single spectrum of wisdom and devotion, as a communion of the Divine with the Divine in which both worshiper and worshiped emerge from the same Ultimate Consciousness. Ramakrishna never preached. For him, each individual's spiritual development is unique: to one person he would suggest a certain approach and to another perhaps the contrary approach. His utterances were ecstatic. His parables are songs for meditation, not rational explanations that constitute any system of theology.

Ramakrishna considered himself a child of Goddess Kali, the Divine Mother of the Universe. As a child who knew nothing and decided nothing, he would speak and act spontaneously as She spoke and acted through him. He did not even regard himself as a guru, or teacher. When holy scholars proclaimed him to be an Avatar, or special emanation of the Divine, Ramakrishna sat among them unself-consciously, intoxicated by the bliss of Divine Presence, half-naked, chew-

ing spices, and repeating, *If you say I am, you must be right,
but I know nothing about it.* However, although *knowing nothing*, this child of the Divine Mother was intensely sensitive.
He responded to subtle changes of psychic and spiritual energy as plants respond to their environment. Once, Ramakrishna was observing from the temple garden two boatmen
exchanging blows far out on the river Ganges. Marks from
these blows appeared immediately on his own body.

The language of Ramakrishna's parables is deceptively
simple. We must be careful not to crystallize this language
or to develop one-sided ideas about his teachings. Ramakrishna often remarked that the most serious distortion of
spiritual life is the one-sidedness which makes us cling exclusively to a particular viewpoint. His guiding vision was
that of the continuum of Consciousness in which all forms
or viewpoints take shape and dissolve like bubbles in a stream.
Ramakrishna's was a comprehensive way of devotion to the
Divine Forms revealed in all sacred traditions. But his was
simultaneously a way of wisdom that never perceived Divine
Forms or Attributes as separate from their source in Ultimate
Consciousness. Ecstatically to experience all forms as one
continuum of Consciousness, which Ramakrishna identified
as Goddess Kali in Her all-embracing aspect, is the Tantric
attitude by which the ways of wisdom and devotion are
fused. Through this Tantric attitude, Ramakrishna helped to
release advanced spiritual seekers from the limits of their
formal practices and religious perspectives into the flow of
Ultimate Consciousness, or Enlightenment.

While certain traditional paths of wisdom insist that the
formless Ground, or Absolute, alone is real and that Divine
and human forms are an illusion, Ramakrishna never makes
such strict demarcation between form and formless, relative
and Absolute. For him the Divine Form, such as Krishna or
Christ does not obscure the formless Absolute, nor is the
Divine Form obliterated in the Absolute. Ramakrishna simply
responded to the stream of Ultimate Consciousness, which
has no intrinsic form yet expresses itself fully through all

sacred traditions and through manifest Being itself. Resembling this universal stream of Consciousness, Ramakrishna flowed freely and reverently through diverse spiritual moods, fully embodying each yet exclusively aligned with none.

The advanced practitioners who encountered Ramakrishna were each strongly identified with a certain traditional approach to the Divine. The first of these was the Brahmani, an adept in the practices of Tantra as well as the Hindu devotional moods in which God is worshiped through the intimate relationships of friend, child, and lover. The Brahmani was a spiritually powerful woman in her fifties when she arrived at the Dakshineswar temple garden where Ramakrishna resided. Looking at him just once as he sat in a blissful mood contemplating his Divine Mother Kali, the Brahmani felt for Ramakrishna the overwhelming attraction a mother feels for her child. That same day, she experienced the culmination of her years of meditation practice.

The Brahmani always carried with her a stone symbol of transcendental Divine Wisdom, which she used for formal worship and meditation. Daily she would cook food and offer it to the Holy Power, which sacramentally manifested itself through the stone. She would then meditate in the radiance of Divine Presence. After encountering Ramakrishna, the Brahmani built her fire by the Ganges and cooked the food to be offered in worship. Ramakrishna, who was dozing in his room on the other side of the temple garden, awakened in a mood of intoxication. He often entered such moods spontaneously as he became responsive to some current of spiritual energy being evoked through authentic worship. He wandered in ecstasy toward the site of the Brahmani's ceremonial offering, arriving just as she completed the invocation. He sat beside the holy stone and began to eat the consecrated food. For a moment the orthodox Brahmani was shocked, but then her spiritual vision opened. She perceived through Ramakrishna a full expression of the Holy Power she had worshiped daily for decades through the medium of the stone symbol. Seated by the river, she entered a deep meditation in which her form, the form of the sacred stone, and the form of Ramakrishna were each revealed as Ultimate Consciousness. Some hours later, she consigned the stone to the waters of the Ganges, realizing that this ritual practice was no longer necessary to evoke Divine Presence. Ramakrishna had released her from the concept of formal worship, fulfilling her spiritual longing by manifesting the sacramental presence through his own person and then becoming transparent to Ultimate Consciousness.

A wandering monk named Jatadhari was another advanced worshiper who came into contact with Ramakrishna. Jatadhari carried with him a small metal image of the child Rama, venerated by Hindus as an incarnation of God. The motherly Jatadhari would not only feed the Holy Child but take it swimming in the Ganges and play tag with it in the fields. His life was totally dedicated to the loving nurture of this child as a form of the Divine. To his illumined vision, the inanimate metal image appeared as a boy of light. He could actually see the child Rama dance and hear him laugh. This highly evolved practitioner could contemplate the spiritual realm not only with eyes closed in deep trance states but also while living daily life. Practitioners of this level have so thoroughly experienced the dreamlike nature of our conventional universe that they encounter the simultaneous presence of alternate universes populated by Divine Forms whose intense purity transforms all experience into devotion and wisdom.

But there is always the danger of becoming confined within one of these alternate universes, forgetting that the ordinary universe is also a manifestation of Holy Power and that no universe exclusively expresses the Divine. Ramakrishna, who released seekers from the confines of any and every world view into the continuum of Consciousness, led Jatadhari out of the realm of this Divine Child in an amusing way. Jatadhari, seated in the temple garden, would notice the Child missing. After anxious search, he would find Ramlala playing with Ramakrishna. Jatadhari was taken aback, for he had encountered no one else who could perceive and play with the spiritual energy focused through the image. More and more, the child Rama played with Ramakrishna. More and more, Jatadhari was left alone, until one day a deep realization dawned. Jatadhari approached Ramakrishna and exclaimed: *I give you this image of Ramlala. I have been worshiping it for many years, and now understand that I need it no longer.* Ramakrishna in no way implied to Jatadhari that his visionary experience had been illusion, but simply fulfilled his spiritual longing. Jatadhari had come to regard Ramakrishna and the Divine Child, as well as his own being, as transparent forms of the same Ultimate Consciousness. This is the Tantric Way, in which form and formless are seen as equivalent. Free from any need for ritual practice, all movements become spontaneous worship, as human forms and various Divine Forms are seen to appear and disappear in the single continuum of Consciousness.

Another advanced practitioner who encountered Ramakrishna was Gangamayi. She was regarded by her devotees as the reincarnation of an attendant of Radha, Krishna's sacred lover, or spiritual consort. Gangamayi's spiritual practice was constant meditation on Radha and her ecstatic love for Krishna. Radha and Krishna are not separate beings seeking union, like ordinary lovers. Krishna and his consort are regarded as emanations of the male and female aspects of the Divine, eternally in perfect union. They play out the drama of separation in human bodies only to reveal the ecstasy of Divine Union through the metaphor of human love. By contemplating Radha and Krishna's dance of love, the worshiper approaches the Divine with a deep longing similar to that experienced by romantic partners intensely attracted to one another. Ramakrishna used to advise seekers to keep constant remembrance of God, as a woman in the midst of an affair thinks about her lover: she goes through her various chores during the day continually contemplating union with her lover, whom she meets at night.

Before encountering Gangamayi, Ramakrishna had engaged in this meditation on Radha's total love for the Divine as Krishna. Gradually the feminine aspect of his nature was awakened, eventually leading to the experience of his mystic identity with Radha. Thus, when he met Gangamayi in the course of a pilgrimage, the two were intensely drawn to one another. Gangamayi recognized Ramakrishna as an embodiment of Radha, on whom she had been meditating intensely for so many years. As the Brahmani and Jatadhari, so Gangamayi was awakened through Ramakrishna's sacramental presence. No longer focusing on the Radha of the past, she experienced her own identity with the immediate spiritual presence of Radha manifest to her fully through Ramakrishna. Ramakrishna, Radha, and her own being were now perceived by Gangamayi as the radiant continuum of Consciousness.

Another dramatic illustration of Ramakrishna's ability to release advanced practitioners from traditional religious forms into Ultimate Consciousness is provided by Gopal Ma. Widowed as a child bride, she had devoted her long life to the worship of baby Krishna as an incarnation of God. She led an existence austere by worldly standards which consisted simply in repetition of the Divine Name and cooking for the Divine Child. Gopal Ma had not attained the visionary level of Jatadhari, who could perceive the living God Child with open eyes, but she felt baby Krishna's invisible presence. One day, she happened to visit Dakshineswar temple garden. Ramakrishna immediately approached her, sat in her lap, and requested her to feed him. His action, as always, was spontaneous and unexpected. His spiritual moods adjusted automatically to the worship of every seeker—in this case, Gopal Ma's highly developed devotion for the Holy Child. Gopal Ma fed Ramakrishna the sweets she had brought to offer at the temple, he thanked her, and she returned to her hermitage on the Ganges. That evening, while engaged in her regular cooking, baby Krishna was suddenly there, appearing in a radiant form that could be seen and touched.

She held the infant in her arms while he ate the food she had prepared. There occurred a perfect interpenetration between the transcendental Divine Realm and the earth plane.

Gopal Ma returned to Ramakrishna early the next morning carrying the Holy Child. She felt an intimate connection between her sudden spiritual awakening and this ecstatic priest of Dakshineswar. The Child crawled onto Ramakrishna's lap, played for a while, disappeared into his body, and re-emerged as light radiates from light. Gopal Ma then began to understand that Ramakrishna was himself an embodiment of Gopala, or baby Krishna, and that Ramakrishna was a being who manifested on various planes of Consciousness simultaneously. For some six months, Gopal Ma continued to live on the transcendental plane with the radiant Child whom she and Ramakrishna alone could perceive. But gradually her visionary experience dissolved, and Ramakrishna in his ordinary human form became her Gopala, whom she would travel to Dakshineswar to feed. Later, another level of realization unfolded which allowed Gopal Ma to perceive all living beings as the baby Krishna and finally as none other than the radiance of Ultimate Consciousness.

Ramakrishna's nature was such that he would merge with and spontaneously embody any authentic religious form he encountered. This process of tangible embodiment of Divine Forms occurs in all sacred traditions. A certain Catholic priest, Padre Pio, lived in southern Italy during the first half of our century. Through the intensity of his meditation on Christ's Passion, this contemporary saint manifested the five wounds, or stigmata, and became a living embodiment of the Christ and His redemptive power. Seekers from all over the world were drawn to this humble monk living in simplicity in his remote monastery, and they received miraculous physical and spiritual healings. Padre Pio's five wounds and their spiritual power are not tales of pious imagination. His stigmata remained fresh for some thirty years, regardless of the healing efforts of modern medical doctors, who, though remaining religious skeptics, reported objectively that the wounds emitted a strong fragrance of lilacs, thus transcending the sphere of ordinary physical lesions.

Figures from sacred myth as well as redemptive figures from oral and recorded history can thus be reconstituted and their power actualized in the being of the holy person, or shaman. Ramakrishna felt an intense longing to re-embody the sacred figures of all traditions, to actualize their spiritual energy through his own person. He took up various Tantric, Yogic, Vaishnava, Vedantic, Islamic, and Christian contemplative practices simply out of his innate thirst to experience Divine Presence through all sacred traditions. He may not have been aware that his practices were going to help re-awaken the inner potency of these various spiritual paths for countless future seekers. He was simply absorbing and re-manifesting forms as the pulsating power of the Goddess alternately withdraws and projects the universe.

Let us consider one other advanced practitioner who came in contact with Ramakrishna and was opened beyond traditional practice into all-embracing Presence. Totapuri was a wandering monk who followed the path of wisdom taught by Advaita Vedanta. All the adepts we have discussed so far were rooted in the devotional experience of Divine Forms, but Totapuri was an adept of the formless Reality, the cloudless sky of the Absolute. He regarded the worship of Divine Forms as childish. Naked and smeared with ashes, Totapuri strolled through Dakshineswar temple garden and noticed Ramakrishna seated there, clapping his hands ecstatically and chanting Mother Kali's Name. Totapuri recognized at once that Ramakrishna, despite his appearance as a simple devotee of the Goddess, was inwardly prepared to receive initiation into the knowledge of the Absolute, in which all forms and all emotions are left behind. Ramakrishna functioned as a mirror. Various advanced practitioners perceived him to be fully prepared in precisely their own contemplative ways. Totapuri approached Ramakrishna with the proposal that he receive initiation into Advaita Vedanta. Ramakrishna replied, *I must ask my Mother Kali.* He entered the temple and received permission from the living Divinity that he experienced pulsating through the stone image enshrined there. That evening, Totapuri began instructing him in formless meditation. But as Ramakrishna concentrated deeply, the radiant figure of the Goddess appeared to his inner eye. When he reported this to Totapuri, the austere naked monk took a sharp stone and pressed it firmly against Ramakrishna's forehead, instructing him to concentrate on the pain and assuring him that he could transcend the Divine Form and merge into the infinite expanse of the Absolute. Once more, Ramakrishna meditated and, as he later expressed it, *with the sword of wisdom, I cut through the Divine Form of Kali.* Her form dissolved, and his individuality completely disappeared into Her formless aspect. For three days Ramakrishna was completely lost to the world, seated in the small meditation hut, motionless, breathing suspended. Totapuri was amazed. He had practiced for forty years to achieve this experience of *nirvikalpa samadhi,* or disappearance of individual identity in the Absolute. This had occurred to Ramakrishna in a single sitting.

Totapuri as an orthodox wandering monk never remained more than three days in one location, but he spent ten months at Dakshineswar because of the intense attraction he felt toward Ramakrishna. During this long stay he contracted serious dysentery. There was prolonged and severe pain, which was distracting Totapuri during meditation. Since he considered the body just a medium, essentially unnecessary after the realization of the Absolute, he decided to give up his body by drowning in the Ganges. The tide was such that he walked far into the river without reaching deep water. When he looked back, he saw the Kali temple gleaming in moonlight and experienced a sudden deep awakening to the presence of the Goddess. He recognized Her as sheer Divine Power and Consciousness, moving through all beings and controlling all events, including his own attempt to discard the body. He now understood the Divine Mother to be the sublime dream power of the Absolute. What he had been calling *maya*, or the mere illusion of forms, was actually the Goddess who projects, nurtures, and dissolves all beings. Totapuri thus accepted the manifest universe and its energy as a radiant expression of the Absolute. The demarcation between form and formless no longer existed for him. He accompanied Ramakrishna to the temple and bowed reverently before the image of Kali. Ramakrishna's mere presence, without any verbal teaching, had opened Totapuri beyond his experience of the formless Absolute into the continuum of Consciousness, from which no Divine, human, or natural forms are excluded and to which no particular doctrine exclusively applies. Totapuri had been transformed by Ramakrishna's Tantric attitude.

Swami Nikhilananda, a disciple of Ramakrishna's wife and a monk of the Ramakrishna Order, describes this Tantric attitude: *The Divine Mother asked Sri Ramakrishna not to be lost in the featureless Brahman but to remain in Bhavamukha, on the threshold of Absolute Consciousness, the borderline between the Absolute and the Relative. . . . Ecstatic devotion to the Divine Mother alternated with serene absorption in the Ocean of Absolute Unity. He thus bridged the gulf between the personal and impersonal, the immanent and transcendent aspects of Reality.* Many spiritual moods flowed through Ramakrishna, but they all appeared and disappeared in the continuum of Consciousness, which is more primal than the personal or the impersonal, the relative or the Absolute, and which he regarded as the Divine Mother in Her ultimate aspect. This ecstatic and unitary understanding of all as Consciousness excludes nothing and establishes no hierarchy. This is the Tantric Way.

Once, while performing the ritual worship of Mother Kali in his capacity as temple priest, Ramakrishna noticed a stray cat. With the milk that was being offered to the Goddess, he fed the cat, which he perceived as simply another manifestation of the Divine Mother or Ultimate Consciousness. Ramakrishna vividly describes this experience: *The Divine Mother revealed to me in the Kali Temple that it was She who had become everything. She showed me that everything was full of Consciousness. The image was Consciousness, the altar was Consciousness, the water vessels were Consciousness, the doorsill was Consciousness. That was why I fed a cat with the food that was to be offered to the Divine Mother. I clearly perceived that all this was the Divine Mother—even the cat.* If we were to develop a metaphysics of the universe in which Ramakrishna was living, it would be based on the axiom that all is Consciousness. This would encompass not only sentient beings but also the crystallized life-energy we call matter. The entire universe, no less than our own mind, is a structuring of Consciousness. As we are capable of perfectly vivid and coherent dreams that we recognize upon waking to have been composed entirely by our dreaming consciousness, so the spiritually awakened person can regard the vividness and coherence of the ordinary world as composed by Ultimate Consciousness alone. This is why Ramakrishna proclaimed that the doorsill and the water vessels were simply Consciousness.

Once, Vivekananda, a close disciple, heard Ramakrishna proclaim that even the clay cup he was drinking from was Brahman, or Ultimate Consciousness. Vivekananda, who had undergone a Western education, became mildly irritated at what he considered an irrational remark and retired to the porch for a smoke. He was conversing with another skeptical disciple about this *nonsense* of a clay cup being Consciousness, when Ramakrishna wandered onto the porch and touched Vivekananda, who at once experienced all physical objects as Consciousness, insubstantial and transparent. The spiritual energy of Ramakrishna's touch was powerful enough to awaken Vivekananda's mind from conventional perception, just as one can be awakened from dream by a touch. Vivekananda's experience is comparable to becoming aware, within the world of the dream, that we are dreaming. All dream objects would still remain visible but would be realized as nothing other than our dream consciousness. The empirical world remained thus transparent to the mystically inebriated young Vivekananda for about three days after this awakening. For his master, Ramakrishna, this was a permanent vision.

Because the implications of Ramakrishna's mystical experiences for the understanding of contemplative life are so rich, we can offer only a glimpse of what appears most significant. And perhaps the most important among Ramakrishna's teachings based on his spiritual experience concerns equal reverence for all sacred traditions as ways to Enlightenment.

To illustrate the plurality of spiritual moods or sacred traditions, Ramakrishna told this parable. The Hindus call that which quenches our thirst *jal*, the Muslims call it *pani*, the English call it *water*. Similarly, each brings a container that is a product of a different culture, and yet they all draw from exactly this same source of refreshment. The clear water of Consciousness, with no shape of its own, perfectly fills all cultural receptacles. Even this analogy could mislead, however, if we concluded that Consciousness is a substance separate from us or from our various receptacles. All is Consciousness. As Ramakrishna expresses it: *God alone is.* This is the ecstatic insight behind the Tantric attitude, which embraces all ways to the Divine as already merged in the Divine.

However, while Ramakrishna taught that all spiritual paths lead to the same goal, the realization of Ultimate Consciousness, he never implied that we should ignore the diversity of spiritual moods and their contrasting cultural expression. Each path or sacred tradition has its own appropriate modes of contemplation, the integrity of which should be respected. When Ramakrishna practiced the constant praise of Allah, into which he was initiated by a wandering Sufi master, he would not enter the Kali temple. After three days of continual absorption in the Holy Name of Allah, Ramakrishna experienced a vision of the Prophet Mohammed, whose radiant form blended with his own and both were revealed as the radiance of Ultimate Consciousness. Ramakrishna experienced a similar communion with the transcendental form of

Jesus following days of continuous Christ-centered contemplation.

Another significant dimension of Ramakrishna's teaching centers around the insight that the universe is neither solid nor permanent but is a dream projection of Ultimate Consciousness. This can easily be misunderstood as a rejection of the world or an escape from responsibility. But Ramakrishna never regarded the dream of relative existence as meaningless, for Divine Presence is continuously being revealed through it, particularly through the life of spiritual aspiration. Our dream of life is a precious treasure, a stream of archetypal images of Ultimate Consciousness. The awakened exploration of this universal dream includes a sense of loving concern for all beings. This is the Tantric Way: all phenomena are to be recognized as the dream-play of Consciousness. Knowing that all is a dream gives one the freedom to move through this single, flowing life as a fish swims gracefully through water. This is the Great Bliss expressed by Tantra through the metaphor of sexual union.

Totapuri, before being released from his exclusive commitment to the formless Absolute, regarded the relative world as *maya*, or senseless illusion, to be renounced totally or ignored as much as possible. But the Tantric practitioner does not reject the world dream. The Tantric Way is to continue to dream the universe, which is Ultimate Consciousness engaged in ecstatic worship of Itself. However, Totapuri's experience of the formless Absolute served as a ripening process for the all-embracing Tantric ecstasy that begins when the practitioner returns from the clear sky of *nirvikalpa samadhi*, the mystical experience in which individuality utterly disappears. The earthly and heavenly facets of the world dream as well as the formless Absolute are now perceived as the same continuum of Consciousness, simultaneously at play and at rest, eternally.

Perhaps the central theme of Ramakrishna's spiritual life was his communion with Goddess Kali. Ramakrishna's last words before his physical death were the repetition of the mantra *Om Kali*, confirming that he was indissolubly related to the Goddess as Her worshiper and as Her emanation. All other Divine Forms, as well as the formless Absolute, Ramakrishna regarded as expressions of Her. This is characteristic of the Tantric Way: the forms of Guru and Chosen Deity—in Ramakrishna's case, Kali Herself is the root Guru—are never obliterated by the experience of the formless or lost sight of in the ecstatic embrace of all forms. Intense devotion for Guru and Deity remains central to the illumined practitioner's spiritual life even in the midst of perfect unitary wisdom. Simultaneously the Tantric practitioner develops a sense of identification with Guru and Deity—the sense of being an emanation of the Deity as well as an eternal worshiper, being the Guru as well as the eternal disciple. On the special feast day of the Goddess, while talking and laughing with his disciples, Ramakrishna would spontaneously assume the *mudra* of Kali, hands raised to bless and to destroy, remaining transfigured for long periods of time, deep in *bhava samadhi*, or absorption in the Deity, oblivious of his human body and the ordinary world. In that mood he would actually become a visible manifestation of Kali, radiating the power of Her blessing, which those present would experience as joy and illumination. This was not a case of possession by the Deity but a temporary revelation of Ramakrishna's own intrinsic Kali nature. Then the mood would pass, and he would again appear as the powerless and playful child of the Divine Mother.

Ramakrishna's veneration of the feminine aspect of the Divine extended to all women, whom he regarded as special manifestations of the Goddess. We notice how important women are in Ramakrishna's life. His wife and first disciple, Sarada Devi, is regarded as his spiritual equal, a twin emanation of Kali. They were a single feminine current of Divine Energy expressed through two bodies. Sarada always regarded her divinely intoxicated husband as the blissful Goddess Herself, not only as a human being. And once, Sarada asked Ramakrishna, *What do you think of me?* Ramakrishna replied, *She who gave me physical birth also appears as the Divine Mother Kali, and you, too, are that same Mother.* Sarada became the spiritual successor of Ramakrishna, guiding his disciples and transmitting visionary power to thousands of seekers after his death.

Mother Kali was the aspect of the Divine that Ramakrishna most often worshiped, not simply as the black, four-armed, ecstatically playful Goddess with whom he could converse face to face, but also as the infinite Womb, the formless Matrix of all forms, the continuum of Consciousness. For Ramakrishna, the Ultimate Consciousness in which all forms appear and disappear was neither masculine nor neuter but distinctly feminine. From the Advaita Vedanta standpoint, the Absolute, called Atman or Brahman, is without gender. But even the staunch Vedantist Totapuri eventually accepted Ramakrishna's worship of the Goddess in order fully to embrace manifest Being as Ultimate Consciousness. This prominence of the feminine principle reflects the Tantric attitude, which regards all women as particularly powerful conduits for the Goddess, transmitting Her power of compassion and wisdom.

Ramakrishna's relation to Goddess Kali was primarily that of child to mother. A clear expression of Ramakrishna's intensely childlike attitude was his powerlessness, his refusal to perform healings and other miracles by exerting psychic and spiritual powers to which he could have had access. *It is all up to the Mother,* he would ecstatically proclaim, *I am simply Her child.* At the end of his life, when he was suffering from throat cancer, his disciples implored him to pray to Goddess Kali to be cured. He demurred, but they insisted. Ramakrishna gives this account of his subsequent conversation with the Divine Mother of the Universe: *I said to Her, "Mother, I cannot swallow food because of my pain. Make it possible for me to eat a little." She pointed you all out to me and said: "What? You are eating enough through all these mouths. Isn't that so?" I was ashamed and could not utter another word.*

Kali thus asked Ramakrishna to identify with all sentient beings as his own being. Identification with all is compassion grounded in the wisdom that perceives the perfect unity of all. Ramakrishna's compassion took the form of intense longing to transmit spiritual energy to authentic lovers of God and, through them, to the entire planet. Ramakrishna would weep and cry out to Mother Kali to send him a few pure and powerful disciples who could receive and hold the Divine Energy that flooded his being. However, in the midst of this intense concern, he perceived that the continuum of Consciousness alone exists, that Consciousness is transmitting only to Consciousness. As Ramakrishna used to exclaim: *I searched for I but found that it is all the Divine Mother.*

CHAPTER THREE

THE WAY OF NATURAL ENLIGHTENMENT

Ramana Maharshi

1879 - 1950

Ramana Maharshi, who lived until 1951, is already regarded as among the classical sages of India. Although he remained in simple rural surroundings and was never strongly influenced by European culture, Ramana lived at the core of awareness from which radiate the languages and images of all cultures. His teaching is uniquely accessible because of the directness of his way to Enlightenment, which is not wedded to Indian culture or to the particular forms of any culture or religion but springs from the primal *I am*, or conscious being, shared naturally by members of every culture.

Ramana's father was a lawyer. There was a certain atmosphere of piety in the household which involved ritualistic worship of various Hindu Gods and Goddesses, but young Ramana underwent no intense religious training. He attended the local Christian school, where sports interested him more than studies and where he was regarded as ordinary and predictable. He had just one unusual characteristic: he was subject to such deep sleep that nothing could rouse him. His boyhood friends would carry him from place to place, or even pummel him as he slept. Hours later he would wake, totally unaware of what had occurred.

Ramana's life continued in a conventional manner until, at the age of sixteen, he read about the lives and practices of the South Indian saints. As a result, he experienced an immediate, though mild, euphoria which lasted several days. He did not interpret this euphoria as a spiritual experience but simply assumed he had a light fever. This was the first tremor of his spiritual awakening.

Several months later, Ramana experienced the sudden opening into Ultimate Consciousness in which his individual identity was almost entirely lost. A family relation had died, and young Ramana decided to explore directly the experience of death. His motive stemmed more from curiosity than any feeling of bereavement. Ramana removed all his clothes, lay on the floor of his room, and with tremendous intensity, imagined his body dead. He closed his eyes, simulating the state of deep sleep. Suddenly there flashed into view, timeless and complete, the primal awareness that lies at the Source of our being, the Ultimate Consciousness that is the Source of Being itself.

This proved not to be an isolated trance. The radiant flow of this primal awareness continued to be experienced throughout Ramana's waking, dream, and dreamless sleep. It was focused in the spiritual center Ramana later called the Heart, two fingers to the right of the breastbone. Still, the boy did not realize he had now become Enlightened. He did not impose any religious interpretation on his spontaneous experience. He simply noticed the blissful flow of primal awareness that went on in the right-hand Heart continuously during the day and at night. Imagine that you are startled. Isolate in your imagination the sudden tingling sensation that flashes through your nervous system. The current of illumination was described by Ramana as a similar sensation but continuous rather than momentary, healing and absorbing rather than shattering or distracting.

For the first few months after his Enlightenment, Ramana often visited the Shiva temple. He had seldom gone there as a child but was now attracted to various temples because, no matter how institutionalized they were, primal awareness was mysteriously focused there. As Ramana stood before the image of Shiva, sometimes he would pray for guidance: where should he go and what should he do now that he perceived the world as inconsequential, perfectly transparent to this Light of primal awareness? At other times he would find no need to pray but would stand silently before the image, experiencing the limitless expanse of Ultimate Consciousness that both he and Shiva equally expressed. Gradually this mood of unity became completely natural to him.

Yet a certain life-pattern remained operative for Ramana, regardless of this condition of complete unity, or illumination. His destiny was to reside at Arunachala Mountain. Ramana experienced a burning sensation in his body which was not alleviated until he left home and, without knowing why, traveled to Arunachala, the holy mountain in South India where for hundreds of years sages and ascetics have lived and practiced. Ramana simply heard the mention of Arunachala, and his body burned until he arrived at this Heart mountain, where he remained, without once leaving, for over fifty years, until his physical death.

When the young Ramana first arrived at Arunachala, he felt no concern whatever for the preservation of the body. He would remain motionless for days at a time, neither eating nor sleeping, totally absorbed in the current of primal awareness from which all phenomena emerge and into which they disappear again like bubbles in a stream. His Enlightenment had not yet begun to direct concern toward living beings, for he now perceived no separate beings or objects, simply the unbroken expanse of Ultimate Consciousness. Ramana was discovered seated in a cave high on the mountain by a wandering holy man who kept him alive by force feeding.

The flowering of compassion and concern occurred spontaneously. The various spiritual practitioners, or *sadhus*, who lived on the mountain assumed that Ramana had taken a vow of silence, because he never spoke. But Ramana had not undertaken any vows. He simply did not think to speak, to eat, or to move, being so absorbed in the awareness of perfect unity. The sadhu who shared Ramana's cave was encountering difficulty with an abstruse passage of scripture. Ramana spontaneously approached him and clearly explained from his own spiritual experience the obscure scriptural meaning. After that, various sadhus and local villagers came to Ramana, who could solve their problems, practical or philosophical, with one or two words, or even through silence. Thus a small ashram, or spiritual community, gathered naturally around Ramana where he lived, high on the mountainside. This growing concern of Ramana to aid others along their way to the experience of unity represents a significant deepening of his original Enlightenment, in which the structure of *self* and *other* had dissolved into pure Consciousness. Now, without obscuring the expanse of perfect unity, individual beings reappeared to Ramana's perception. These individuals, although naturally rooted in primal awareness, were ignorant of their Source and therefore in need of Ramana's concern and personal assistance.

While Ramana preferred to remain high on the mountainside, difficult of access, he was eventually brought down to the foot of the mountain, where he would fulfill his destiny by becoming known throughout India and the world. His return, indicating yet a further deepening of Enlightenment, occurred in this way. Ramana's mother, who had been seeking her son since his disappearance from the household, heard of a young sadhu living high on the slopes of Arunachala. She made the arduous journey, recognized her child, and remained with him as his disciple, being inspired to lead the contemplative life by Ramana's powerful, silent presence. One day, she died. As she took her last breaths, Ramana kept his hands on her head and her heart, guiding her through subtle psychic realms, clearing from her way various obstacles to the experience of perfect unity. With this potent assistance, she attained *mukti*, or release into Ultimate Consciousness. She was therefore accorded a saint's burial at the foot of the mountain. Ramana used to walk down the mountain every day to spend some time at her tomb. One day, about six months after she died, Ramana strolled down the mountain and settled permanently there by the tomb, which he did not regard as the physical remains of his human mother but as a shrine to the Divine Mother of the Universe. Arunachala Mountain embodied Shiva, or Divine Transcendence; the mother's tomb embodied Shakti, or Divine Immanence, which is experienced in Hindu tradition as feminine. As Arunachala, or Shiva, had first drawn Ramana from his family home, so Shakti, or the Feminine Divine, drew Ramana to Her through the instrument of his human mother, making him available to humanity at large. Now that Ramana was accessible, a large ashram began to build up around him at the foot of the holy mountain.

Although he was the central focus for decades in an ashram visited by thousands of seekers from all over the world, Ramana never recognized anyone as his disciple. Many considered themselves his disciples and all took spiritual instruction from him, but Ramana declared unequivocally that no one was his disciple. He would tirelessly insist that Ultimate Consciousness alone is the Guru, or teacher. The Guru is simply the primal awareness focused two fingers to the right of the breastbone and accessible through the primordial sense, *I am*. Ramana explained that while we are aware of the body, the source of the *I am* is experienced in what he called the right-hand Heart, but if our attention becomes totally absorbed in the stream of primal awareness, all sense of an individual body dissolves and no exclusive location remains. Primal awareness, or Ultimate Consciousness, is then understood to be situated nowhere and everywhere.

Often, when we instinctively point to ourselves, to the *I* or the *me*, we find our index finger approaching the right center of the chest. Even those who are left-handed usually point to the right side. Ramana once experienced a clear yogic demonstration of this right-hand Heart. He was walking on the mountainside with some friends and suddenly perceived a light move from the left of his chest to the right. He fell down paralyzed, breath suspended, his body turning blue.

For some minutes there were no physical signs of life. His heart had stopped. Ramana could not speak but could hear his friends bemoaning his death. He was perfectly awake and perceived his awareness radiating from the right side of the chest. Then, as Ramana reports, there was a flash as one spark of this universal conscious Light leaped from the right side to the left side, igniting his physical heart into activity once more. Ramana later made use of certain Indian religious and philosophical language to express his basic spiritual insight but always assumed that his revelatory experience of the right-hand Heart was self-authenticating.

Spiritual guide

Ramana did indicate, however, that although the Guru, or teacher, is within everyone as primal awareness, an illumined sage can push us in the direction he described as *inward* in the sense of being more primary, or primal. Ramana could give this initiatory push by touch or by glance. Seated in silence, he would suddenly turn, fix one with an intense gaze, and the person would become directly aware of the right-hand Heart and its vibrant current of primal awareness. Those who experienced the power of Ramana's gaze have reported that the initiation was so clear and vivid they could never again seriously doubt that the Guru was none other than their own primal conscious being.

Ramana could also initiate by dream. There are instances of persons having dreams of him gazing into their eyes. Ramana did not consider himself as separate from these dreamers but as their own primal awareness, providing them with potent clues to Self-realization. In certain instances, however, he actually bilocated and projected his presence not into the dream but into the waking state of the seeker, through the power of conscious dreaming, for which the waking state is simply another dream state—*dream one* and *dream two*, as Ramana used to call them. Ramana tells of an experience of bilocation in which he left his ordinary physical body in the ashram and at the same time found himself walking along a road hundreds of miles distant. He entered a temple and recognized that one of his followers was meditating there. The seeker was evoking Ramana and this had attracted Ramana to project himself there in order to intensify the spiritual practice of this sincere meditator, who looked up and actually perceived Ramana's luminous figure. However, Ramana never made extensive use of such psychic powers, because he was not interested in manipulating the events of our waking dream but in awakening the seeker to primal awareness, which is prior to the states of dreaming and waking, prior to birth and death. His initiatory activity was entirely motivated by the concern that had awakened suddenly in that high mountain cave, the compassionate concern to guide all conscious beings into their ever-present Source.

Ramana's compassion was instinctive and far-reaching. Once, after the ashram had become large, he noticed that only the more regular visitors who sat near him in the dining hall would be offered coffee. Without remarking on it he simply declined ever to drink coffee again. This is not compassion in the emotional or sentimental sense but an intense living of the lives of all beings as our own life, an insight into the unity of all life as Ultimate Consciousness at play through countless forms. Ramana's compassion extended to animals and human beings equally. He even declared, although the view is completely unorthodox in the context of Indian philosophy, that an animal can achieve Self-realization, or Enlightenment. A certain cow used to come each morning to greet Ramana, spend the day grazing, and return spontaneously at twilight to bid him good night. When she died, Ramana placed his hands on the cow's head and heart, as he had done with his mother, guiding the animal through the illusions of separateness and multiplicity. Ramana confirmed that the cow had attained release into Ultimate Consciousness, and she was accorded a saint's burial.

Ramana's compassion also poured out for less spiritually evolved members of the animal kingdom. A dog was chasing a squirrel. Ramana saw the situation, turned suddenly, and threw his staff between them. This distracted the dog long enough that the squirrel escaped, but Ramana fell and broke his own collarbone. This self-sacrifice was completely spontaneous. Perfectly merged in the one Consciousness, not only as transcendence but also as immanence, Ramana simply experienced the squirrel's suffering as his own.

The spiritual teachings of Ramana Maharshi do not include certain traditional religious attitudes that are often thought necessary. The need for some Divinity or Absolute separate from oneself was superfluous to him. Enlightenment can spring up, as Ramana would say, directly from the ground of the *I am* by concentrating on this word that we use so often: *I, I, I*. The *I am* is not to be regarded as necessarily self-centered or limiting but as our central mode of access to Ultimate Consciousness. One should not contemplate any assertion of the form *I am this* or *I am that* but simply the primal intuition *I am*, which is prior to all assertions.

Ramana's method for awakening into primal awareness, or awareness at its Source, is called *vichara*, which simply means inquiry. It consists of continuously asking, and eventually living, the existential question: *Who is it that is having this particular thought or perception I am now having?* or, more simply, *Who am I?* The purpose of the questioning is not to isolate an individual *I* but to trace the rootedness of the separate *I* in the universal *I am*, which itself ultimately dissolves into primal awareness. This dynamic approach is without any form and without any particular intellectual or emotional content. Ramana was asked, for example, whether a seeker should meditate on the Vedantic affirmation *I am He* in order to evoke the experience of unity with the Divine. Ramana replied, *Find out first who it is that meditates on "I am He."* Thus vichara undercuts any possible content and any conceptual or doctrinal framework by asking, *Who is speaking?* regardless of the particular cultural or spiritual language being spoken.

Year after year Ramana sat in the meditation hall of the ashram, receiving all visitors and instructing them in vichara. Ramana would remain silent for many hours, either with eyes closed in contemplation of the transcendent aspect of Consciousness or gazing out the window in contemplation of Consciousness as immanence. During these periods of silence, the visitors and residents would sit in Ramana's powerful presence, tracing their own primal awareness with eyes open or closed by inquiring, *Who am I?* Then Ramana would initiate or intensify the process of vichara in those present by his gaze and respond to questions, always redirecting the questioner to the root inquiry, *Who am I?*

Ramana did not regard the practice of *Who am I?* as a formal meditation technique but as an attitude that should quietly permeate daily consciousness. However, he did encourage beginners to sit for formal meditation morning and evening in order to help continue vichara throughout the waking state and even during dream. After one penetrates deeply enough into inquiry, a natural flow is discovered and inquiry happens spontaneously. The increasing gravitational force of primal awareness intensifies the *Who am I?* as we approach closer to the core of ordinary awareness. Ramana says, *The quest for the Self of which I speak is a direct method, for the moment you really get into the quest and begin to go deeper, the real Self is waiting there to receive you, and then whatever is to be done is done by something else, and you as an individual have no hand in it.*

To those, not drawn to pure vichara, who wished to use mantra or prayer, Ramana suggested practicing vichara simply by tracing the source of the mantra or prayer, inquiring *Who is praying?* Therefore, although intrinsically independent of any verbal formulation, vichara can be carried on effectively in conjunction with traditional religious practices. Yet Ramana's teachings tend to move us beyond religious imagery, directly to its Source. We may spend years visualizing Divine Forms in our prayer or meditation, eventually to realize that these are none other than potent manifestations of primal awareness. For Ramana, direct investigation of the roots of our own awareness was preferred. After experiencing all as Ultimate Consciousness, if we are still drawn to the traditional worship of Christ or Krishna, then such worship is our karmic destiny, the flow of primal awareness through our particular pattern or grain. Ramana himself had a clear karmic destiny. He was linked with the mountain Arunachala as a manifestation of Shiva, or transcendent Wisdom. He was compelled to go there. Similarly, Ramakrishna was linked with Divine Mother Kali as manifest at the Dakshineswar temple garden. We all have some deep karmic pattern which Indian philosophy interprets as impressions from our previous lifetimes but which could also be understood as the interplay of spiritual archetypes focusing through us. When we advance in vichara, these patterns of manifestation do not simply disappear. The forms, the places, the spiritual languages continue to appear but do not interrupt the life of vichara, which is fundamentally formless, placeless, and silent.

The approach of vichara, since it is total and constant tends to run counter to all formal rules. Ramana remarks: *Regulation of life, such as getting up at a fixed hour, bathing, repetition of a mantra, observing ritual, all this is for people who are not drawn to vichara. But for those who can practice this method, all rules and discipline are unnecessary.* Since *Who am I?* is not designed for deliberate contemplation, one should move from asking to living the question *Who am I?* Eventually one arrives at the point where this inquiry is not a deliberate mental act but part of the flow of daily awareness, continually and naturally reorienting itself toward its Source as primal awareness. As one checks the clock, the inquiry naturally arises *Who is telling time?* As one opens a book, awareness spontaneously inquires, *Who is reading?* Thus daily activity is not inhibited but gradually rendered transparent to Ultimate Consciousness.

The *Who am I?* is an underlying attitude, not a mantra to repeat over and over again. Ramana often playfully remarked that if one insists upon repeating a mantra, the best mantra is *I, I, I*—playfully, because this is what we are already doing. However, the point is not to reinforce this *I* as a specific personal being, as we ordinarily do, but to reveal the Source of the *I am*, which is inexpressible, because it has no form or quality but simply *is*. Someone asked Ramana whether there was ever an answer to *Who am I?* and he replied, *You just stop questioning*. The Consciousness that asks the question is already the answer.

Vichara is characterized by Ramana as attenuation of ego. Ego creates various melodic lines against the hum or drone of primal awareness. When listening to Indian classical music, Ramana reports, his main attention naturally focused on the rich underlying drone rather than on the melody. In the unillumined state, we hardly notice the profoundly integrating tone ef primal awareness, because we are distracted by the play of ego. Self-realization, or Enlightenment, is the rediscovery of this peaceful hum of conscious being as a single eternal flow, which does not eliminate the countless melodic lines but harmonizes and grounds them.

Ramana used the term *mind* synonymously with *ego*, and spoke about the disappearance of mind, which simply means awakening to primal awareness. Ramana often remarked that the sage's mind is like the moon in a daytime sky. The sage does not need the moonlight to see, because the sun of primal awareness is shining. At the same time, the sage is clearly aware of the daytime moon, or mind, and refers to the mind in conventional mundane matters. As the source of the moon's reflected light is the sun, so the source of the mind's thought and perception is primal awareness. Disappearance of the mind, therefore, is simply attending to the source of the mind's reflected light and need not involve loss of ability to think and to perceive.

The transcendence of mind or ego, however, cannot be undertaken directly or willfully, for this would immediately reinvolve the ego, which is, as Ramana often joked, like the thief acting as policeman in order to apprehend himself. Rather than battling the worldly ego with a more intense spiritual ego, Ramana counsels us to *scorch the ego by ignoring it.* One scorches the ego by seeing into its intrinsic emptiness, its nature as mere reflection. Moonlight is nothing other than reflected sunlight, and in this sense there is no moonlight. As Ramana teaches: *Instead of setting about saying there is a mind or an ego and I want to kill it, you must begin to seek its source and find that it does not exist at all. . . . When the mind unceasingly investigates its own nature it transpires that there is no such thing as mind. This is the direct path for everyone . . . the fact is that the mind is only a bundle of thoughts. . . . Find its source and hold on to it. The mind will fade away of its own accord.* Thus the practitioner of vichara walks slowly and persistently toward the mirage of separate ego, which at first seems to recede intact, and then simply fades away. Orientation to the Source of the *I am* gradually and naturally dissolves the mirage of distractions, enabling us to perceive the endlessly flowing and refreshing stream of primal awareness.

Vichara goes to the root of all contemplative practices. For instance, concerning the yogic form of contemplation, *I am not the body, I am not the mind, I am not the senses,* Ramana remarked, *In order to be able to say "I am not this," there must be the I to say it. . . . The I-thought is the root thought. If the root is pulled out, all the rest is at the same time uprooted.* No particular assertions or negations are necessary in order to return to that primal ground, that Ultimate Consciousness which we already are. Yet we are often tempted to engage in some form of analysis, forgetting to inquire, *Who is analyzing?* A visitor asked Ramana, *Suppose I have the thought "horse" and I try to trace its source. I find that it is due to memory and the memory in turn is due to prior perception of the object "horse."* Ramana replied, *Who asked you to think about all that? All those are also thoughts. What good will it do you to go on thinking about memory and perception? That I which has the perception of memory . . . find that out.* Thus vichara is more direct than psychological analysis, both Eastern and Western, because it does not rely primarily on articulation. And vichara is even more direct than most contemplative techniques, which, if not analytic in nature, may rely on imagination and thus do not focus directly on the primal awareness prior to all articulation. Whatever form of contemplation we practice, we must eventually inquire, *Who is practicing?*

Yet vichara, precisely because unsupported by intellectual or emotional articulation, can he painfully difficult to sustain. Constant vichara resembles the attempt to remain awake for days at a time. The sleepiness that overwhelms us in this attempt is distraction from the Source of awareness by the various objects or structures of awareness. This path of staying awake to primal awareness, which Ramana characterized as most direct and simple, is perhaps the most demanding practice of all.

We now move from the consideration of Ramana's teaching *Who am I?* to the natural Enlightenment which this approach presupposes. One does not continually inquire *Who am I?* to attain some miraculous superawareness but to awaken into the Ultimate Consciousness, which already constitutes everyday thought and perception. Ramana's realization is simply this: Enlightenment is never absent. We already are primal awareness. This very mind that is now thinking and reading is none other than Ultimate Consciousness, the Ground of Being. As long as we withhold our full assent to such an affirmation, we must continue spiritual practice and wait. But when we can feel honestly at home with the attitude that the ultimate goal is attained, and has always been attained, this is the dawn of Self-realization.

The return to the original clarity of Ultimate Consciousness is comparable to a game of chess in which we must gradually sacrifice all our pieces in order to open ourselves to checkmate, or Enlightenment. This process of clearing away leaves nothing to be thought or perceived. As Ramana tells his listeners, *Meditation helps to overcome the illusion that the Self, or Atman, is something to see.* There is nothing to see, only to be. Ramana often asked: *How do you recognize yourself now? Do you need a mirror?* One does not even have to inquire, *Who am I?* Experiment now. Close your eyes. As particular sensations subside, the body blends into the general sensory background. For a few moments at least, the mind may not break into habitual patterns of thinking. Balance here in simple awareness. Do you require any mirror, name, or concept to point to yourself now? This primal awareness *is* you, as well as all sentient beings. This is Ultimate Consciousness, the goal of all sacred quest. All spiritual practice is preparing or purifying us to be able to remain continuously as this simple Presence.

We need not close our eyes. That was simply an aid to the contemplative experiment. Repeat the same process with eyes open. Feel awareness radiating from the primal *I am*, gradually flowering into thinking and perceiving. Now turn from this articulation to its Source. No further authentication of primal awareness is necessary. Neither are there two selves, higher and lower, absolute and relative. There is only Consciousness. Says Ramana, *Consciousness is the Self of which everyone is aware. No one is ever away from his Self and therefore everyone is in fact Self-realized. Only, and this is the great mystery, people do not know this and want to realize the Self.*

Yet this mysterious desire to realize the Self, to be completely and continuously conscious of Consciousness, is rare and precious. Perhaps most persons, unless probed deeply, would not admit to any desire to awaken into primal awareness. However, all human beings are seeking fulfillment, and sages from various cultures teach that the fundamental root of this search is the longing to experience Ultimate Consciousness or, in another mystical language, to taste of union with the Divine. Yet a gradual ripening process is needed to make the transition between instinctive longing for fulfillment and disciplined spiritual commitment.

When we consciously turn toward Enlightenment as a goal, ironically we separate ourselves from it. In our longing to attain the Ultimate, inadvertently we project the goal far beyond our present awareness, whereas Ultimate Consciousness is already here, sustaining the ordinary function of mind and senses. Even after the aspiration to Enlightenment awakens, we will travel along countless byways before returning home to primal awareness. This process of spiritual evolution is a house of mirrors. Knowing that we must move through a mirror maze does not help to discover the shortest path. We will have to explore various corridors, colliding with mirrored walls that appear to be open doors.

But even as we are undergoing this process of spiritual development, which may appear as a game of chess or a maze, we should affirm Ramana's basic realization that we are naturally Enlightened. Ramana once remarked: *Realization consists only in getting rid of the false idea that one is not realized.* When liberated from this false notion by Ramana's illumined affirmation, we recognize Consciousness itself to be the ultimate fulfillment that human beings have endlessly sought. Our daily consciousness is intrinsically Ultimate Consciousness. This insight, which is the dawning of Enlightenment, need not change any appearing structures. One need not be transformed from a lawyer working in the city to a monk or nun meditating in the mountains. No form of creativity is inhibited by the realization that the goal of all life has always been attained as primal awareness. Life is now no longer regarded primarily as evolution but as play.

But even after Enlightenment, there remains our karmic destiny, our particular energy pattern, our grain. Each being has its own special momentum or motivation. This is why the relative universe continues to manifest. Our karmic momentum may lead us, for instance, to reshape society. But we should realize that although there is no ultimate society, this very Consciousness that we use to design social institutions is intrinsically ultimate.

When Ramana spoke, he either instructed seekers in the

practice of *Who am I?* or evoked his deepest realization: the natural Enlightenment of all beings. When he remained silent, absorbed in primal awareness, his presence both instructed seekers in vichara and fully expressed the fact of natural Enlightenment, which exists prior to any spiritual practice. Ramana teaches: *You speak of various paths as if you were somewhere and the Self were somewhere else and you had to go and attain it. But in fact the Self is here and now and you are it always. It is like being here at the ashram and asking people the way to Ramana Ashram and then complaining that each one shows a different path and asking which one to follow.* This remark enables us to understand more deeply Ramakrishna's conviction that all spiritual paths lead to the same goal. The paths are illusory, and this, ironically, is why they are fundamentally in harmony. There are no separate paths. There is only Consciousness itself, which is always present and thus cannot be described as a goal. What we thought were paths to a goal are just the playfulness of Ultimate Consciousness. Any spiritual path we follow is an illusion, because, as a path, it purports to lead us away from where we are, whereas Consciousness is always here. But we can travel spiritual paths, joyfully knowing them to be illusory, or provisional, as Ramana often venerated the holy mountain Arunachala by circumambulation, a path of worship that is, appropriately, circular in form.

Various spiritual practices impart their own flavor to Self-realization, or Enlightenment. Goddess Kali, as a Divine Form assumed by Ultimate Consciousness, imparted Her lasting fragrance to the illumined being of Ramakrishna, who repeated Her mantra with his last breath. Similarly, circumambulation and praise of the holy mountain remained a form of veneration for the illumined Ramana until his death. The presence of Kali, or Arunachala, can persist for these Enlightened beings precisely because such Divine Forms are not intrinsically separate from primal awareness. Their nature is dreamlike, but their reality is more archetypal than the dream of space and time. They are comparable to the transendental Forms of Plato's philosophy, living principles whose mode of being is indestructible because it is not substantial in any physical sense. We cannot dissolve a geometrical theorem. And countless systems of geometry, each with contrasting axioms, can subsist simultaneously. They do not impede each other. This is the nature of the various spiritual paths. They are intrinsically transparent to the Ultimate Consciousness at their Source.

Let us consider Ramana Maharshi's death. At seventy, he developed a tumor on his arm which was operated on several times without anesthetic. Ramana tried to clarify the meaning, or lack of meaning, of pain and illness for the totally illumined person: *They take this body for Ramana and attribute suffering to him. What a pity! Where is pain if there is no mind?* The approach of Ramana was not that of the healer who removes pain but that of the sage who perceives all phenomena, including pain, as Ultimate Consciousness. Years before, Ramana had elucidated this point: *If the hand of the jnani, or knower of truth, were cut with a knife, there would be pain as with anyone else, but because his mind is in bliss, he does not feel the pain as acutely as others do.* Thus ordinary bodily experience does exist for the illumined sage, although greatly muted.

When begged by some devotees to cure himself with yogic powers, Ramana replied in the spirit of vichara: *Who is there to have such a thought? Who is there to will this?* When near death, Ramakrishna received this same request from his devotees. Rather than responding immediately, as Ramana did, from the standpoint of unitary insight, Ramakrishna agreed to ask his Divine Mother Kali. He went to the temple and humbly requested, *Mother, please let me eat a little in order to keep the body together.* Goddess Kali replied, *You are eating through all mouths. Why do you have to eat through this mouth?* The same truth is being expressed through both these revelatory media: the Source Consciousness of Ramana and the Divine Mother of Ramakrishna. The Source and the Mother are the same primal awareness.

During his final illness, various devotees of Ramana continued to plead that they needed his physical presence to help them in their spiritual practice. Ramana replied, *You attach too much importance to the body. They say that I am dying, but I am not going away: where would I go? I am here.* Ramana, like any illumined being, is everywhere. He is with us now as we think about him. Ramana *is* the Ultimate Consciousness that we are. And we are Ramana. His life is an expression of our own deepest Life. His story is essentially our own awakening.

The physical death occurred on April 14, 1951. Some devotees outside his room were singing at dusk one of Ramana's own hymns to Shiva as the mountain Arunachala. On hearing the song, writes an eyewitness, *Ramana's eyes opened and shone. He gave a brief smile of indescribable tenderness.* This was the poignant tenderness of a mother for her children. The devotees were singing as spiritual children to the mountain Arunachala, which Ramana knew to be actually their own primal awareness. The eyewitness continues: *From the outer edges of his eyes tears of bliss rolled down. One more deep breath and no more. There was no struggle, no other sign of death, only that the next breath did not come.*

Cartier-Bresson, the French photographer, had come to the ashram the week before. He tells the following remarkable experience at the hour of Ramana's death: *I saw a shooting star with a luminous tail unlike any I have ever seen before moving slowly across the sky and reaching the top of Arunachala, the mountain, disappearing behind it. We immediately looked at our watches. It was 8:47. We raced to the ashram only to find that the master had passed into Mahanirvana at that exact minute. Nor was this experience only documented by a select few. . . . All the English and Tamil papers which arrived this morning from Madras referred to the meteor which had been seen in the sky over the entire state of Madras at 8:47 on the night of April 14, by a large number of people in different places. These eyewitnesses had been struck by its peculiar look and behavior.* Was this an ordinary meteor or was Ramana simply dreaming this brilliant presence into the collective dream of our waking state as his last tribute to Arunachala, as his last act of worship or circumambulation of the holy mountain? Responds Ramana: *Who is asking this question?*

CHAPTER FOUR

TEN SEASONS OF ENLIGHTENMENT

Zen Ox-herding

Enlightenment is not an isolated attainment of ancient or legendary sages but a process flowering through members of every culture, a process in which our consciousness gradually becomes transparent to its own intrinsic nature. Various traditions have developed subtle languages to describe phases of this process. These dimensions of Enlightenment are not scholastic projections; they reflect the complex tissue of awareness as it gradually becomes purified or clarified by awareness of itself.

The seeker of Enlightenment must become as close an observer of consciousness as the Eskimo is of snow condition. Enlightenment is not simply an expanse of whiteness any more than snow is, but a process developing through various seasonal changes. Ten seasons of Enlightenment are evoked by the Ox-herding pictures, evolved in twelfth-century China, in which the spiritual quest is depicted as the search for an elusive Ox that roams wild in the rain forest. This Ox symbolizes the intrinsic nature of consciousness, the mystery of what we are. In Buddhist teaching, our intrinsic nature is revealed to be that we have no intrinsic nature, that is, the essence of our consciousness is void, free, or open. The dimensions of Enlightenment suggested by these ten pictures become progressively more comprehensive as this essence of consciousness, or what Zen masters call our *True Nature*, becomes clearer and clearer.

The first Ox-herding picture, or phase of Enlightenment #1 is called Seeking the Ox. This marks the moment when we become explicitly aware of the process of Enlightenment. We now imagine the mystery of our True Nature to be an object of search. Prior to Seeking the Ox, our spiritual growth has occurred in the disguise of ordinary life, for all desires express in more or less clarified ways the longing for ultimate fulfillment, or Enlightenment. Now we have become formal spiritual seekers, a development that is indispensable for focusing our conscious energy toward True Nature. Yet this development also involves a fundamental illusion which Zen tradition exposes in an uncompromising way. We read from the traditional commentary on the Ox-herding pictures: *The Ox has really never gone astray. So why search for it?* By seeking our True Nature, we are creating an illusory duality between the one who seeks and the object that is sought. Why search for True Nature, which is already present as the consciousness by which one carries out the search? Our True Nature is never lost and therefore can never be found. We cannot discover a satisfactory answer to the puzzle *Why search?* and this not-finding-an-answer brings about the gradual cessation of search which is the flowering of Enlightenment.

The ancient commentary continues: *Having turned his back on his true nature, the man cannot see it. Because of his defilements he has lost sight of the Ox. Suddenly he finds himself confronted by a maze of crisscrossing paths.* The seeker is pictured wandering through a mountainous jungle or rain forest. The maze of paths represent the complex possibilities for thought and action in any given culture and within each individual. The seeker assumes that the Ox has taken one of these ways or byways, but no matter how sincerely he follows the various paths, he will never find the Ox of True Nature along any particular path. The Ox is eventually understood to be the entire maze of paths, the infinite rain forest as well as the seeker who wanders through it. Our True Nature is none other than the fundamental principle of Being which Zen masters also speak of as *Original Mind*. The commentary describes this illusory quest for the Original Mind, which can never be lost but from which we have turned away: *Desolate through forests and fearful in jungles he is seeking an Ox which he does not find. Up and down dark, nameless, wide-flowing rivers in deep mountain thickets he treads many bypaths.* There is exhilaration and adventure at this stage of search, yet also a growing sense of desolation and even despair. The seeker has left behind ordinary desires only to become lost in transcendental ambition. This is an impossible quest for the concept of quest itself obscures the True Nature which we seek and which is not beyond our own present seeing or hearing. The commentary on this first Ox-herding picture ends suggestively: *At evening he hears cicadas chirping in the trees.* The music of the cicadas provides a subtle clue to the seeker's True Nature. This humming sound pervades the jungle as Original Mind pervades all the structures of seeking. The seeker is exploring the trackless wilderness, frustrated and weary, but the soothing song of the cicadas is omnipresent, subtly permeating all dimensions of his mind and senses.

The second Ox-herding picture, or phase of Enlightenment is called Finding the Tracks. The commentary reads: *Through the Sutras and teachings he discerns the tracks of the Ox. He has been informed that, just as differently shaped golden vessels are all basically the same gold, so each and every thing is a manifestation of the Self. He has not actually entered the gate, but he sees in a tentative way the tracks of the Ox.* The tracks are the wisdom teachings, expounded by various illumined beings, that the sound of the cicadas, and indeed all phenomena, are the same light of Original Mind, or True Nature. The seeker now becomes the finder, but as there was illusion inherent in the seeking so is there illusion in the finding. The tracks of the Ox are none other than the seeker's own tracks through his own consciousness.

Innumerable footprints he has seen in the forest and along the water's edge. Over yonder does he see the trampled grass? Signs of the Ox's presence are noticed everywhere. The forest no longer seems desolate. Yet, following these tracks will not lead anywhere because, as the commentary continues, *Even the deepest gorges or the topmost mountains cannot hide this Ox's nose, which reaches right to Heaven.* The Ox is the entire realm of Consciousness that seekers of the first stage and beginning practitioners of the second stage are exploring, leaving their own tracks everywhere. However, following these tracks is a fruitful and indispensable illusion, without which the seeker would not be drawn deeper into the actual practice of meditation on the intrinsic nature of all phenomena as Original Mind. Children often need to be presented with an incomplete picture to move them in the right direction.

The third Ox-herding picture is called First Glimpse of the Ox. The commentary expands on what was hinted by the song of cicadas: *If he will but listen intently to everyday sounds, he will come to realization and at that instant see the very Source.* The noise of city traffic is the Ox bellowing. This encounter with the Ox does not come through hearing esoteric teaching or the abstract contemplation of the sutras but through direct experience. No longer is the Ox imagined to be somewhere out in the jungle. As the commentary suggests: *The six senses are no different from this true Source.* Any of our sense perceptions or thoughts can become a glimpse of the Ox. The commentary continues: *In every activity, the Source is manifestly present. When the inner vision is properly focused, one comes to realize that which is seen as identical with the true Source.* The practitioner who has glimpsed the Ox is consciously Enlightened, for he or she is no longer seeking the Ox or finding its tracks. The Ox is known to be omnipresent, not in abstract contemplation but in direct experience. Reflects the commentary: *The nightingale warbles on a twig, the sun shines on undulating willows. There stands the Ox. Where could he hide?* The Source cannot hide, because it exists through all forms, though they differ in structure and appearance as suns, nightingales, and willows. Yet this third phase of Enlight-

enment provides only an inebriating glimpse, an ecstatic realization which comes and goes. Further struggle and discipline
are required to expand and stabilize such flashes of insight.

The fourth Ox-herding picture is Catching the Ox. *Today
he encountered the Ox, which has long been cavorting in the wild
fields, and actually grasped it. For so long a time has it reveled in
these surroundings that the breaking of its old habits is not easy.
It continues to yearn for sweet-scented grasses: it is still stubborn
and unbridled. If he would tame it completely the man must use
his whip. He must tightly grasp the rope and not let it go, for the
Ox still has unhealthy tendencies.* The intransigent character of
the Ox experienced in this stage is expressed literally in Japanese as *wild strength.* This is the raw energy of Enlightenment for which nothing matters, the complete abandon that
perceives creation and destruction as one. Such energy must
be tempered and refined, a function of advanced spiritual
disciplines which cannot begin until one has generated profound insight into the omnipresence of Original Mind. For,
prior to such insight, spiritual disciplines are simply an
expression of the illusion of seeking. We must now hold and
embrace the Ox, sustain our perception of True Nature with
such disciplines as total compassion, perfect nonviolence,
unwavering truthfulness. These are the *whip* and *rope.* We
are dealing with the wild strength of the Ox, which can prove
dangerous. Distortions of genuine spirituality are possible at
this stage. If discipleship and disciplined practice are prematurely abandoned, the energy of Enlightenment can dissipate into arbitrary and self-willed activity. That the Ox is
still stubborn and unbridled and *yearns for sweet grasses* reflects
the fact that primal awareness has been eternally at play in
an infinite field unlimited by human conventions. The conventional surface thinking that operates our daily lives has
developed as a byroad, apparently partitioned from the open
field of True Nature. When this illusory partition is broken
through and the wild Ox enters into conventional human
awareness, the advanced practitioner's system of values and
even his physical nervous system must be reconstituted so

as to harmonize the energy of Enlightenment with personal and cultural being.

The fifth Ox-herding picture, Taming the Ox, indicates a more intense intimacy with True Nature. The previous phase, Catching the Ox, is to sustain and control spiritual insight under all conditions. Taming the Ox is more subtle. An effortless intimacy or friendship with the Ox is now being established. All movement of thought is to be integrated into the realization of True Nature. All phenomena are *tamed* by the childlike friendliness of the one who is ceasing to be an advanced practitioner by becoming an illumined sage. Reads the commentary: *With the rising of one thought, another and another are born. Enlightenment brings the realization that such thoughts are not unreal, since even they arise from our True Nature. It is only because delusion still remains that they are imagined as unreal.* We might suppose that Taming the Ox would begin by the elimination of all thoughts, or at least certain thoughts regarded as negative, impure, or unreal. But that is not the way of Enlightenment, which operates fundamentally by inclusion rather than by exclusion. Taming the Ox is the unlearning by the practitioner of convictions concerning discipline, purity, and discrimination that were important in earlier stages. When we follow the tracks of the Ox, which appear as the teachings of various sacred traditions, we learn to discriminate between the unreal and the real, between our inveterate human illusions and the wisdom of the sages. Now we discover all thoughts to be intrinsically the same, since they each arise from Original Mind. Only because traces of illusion remain is any thought imagined to be different from Enlightenment. Yet without this provisional spiritual illusion of discrimination between ultimate truth and relative truth, between insight and ignorance, there would have been no clarification of True Nature but only the chaos of ordinary desire.

Taming the Ox begins to dissipate this illusory discrimination between spiritual life and ordinary life, a distinction that is no longer useful. The one who is becoming a sage makes friends with the limitations of the ordinary ego rather than withdrawing into the transcendental ego of the spiritual seeker or advanced practitioner. This is the first hint of the mysterious ordinariness into which the sage eventually disappears. Describing the Ox at this stage, the commentary reads: *Properly tended, it becomes clean and gentle. Untethered it willingly follows its master.* The point of this taming is to untether the Ox, to release the primal awareness which we have focused as a particular body and mind. The Ox becomes a free companion, not a tool for plowing the field of Enlightenment. This is a graceful process, not a violent unleashing of energy. All movement becomes balanced.

The sixth Ox-herding picture, or phase of Enlightenment, is Riding the Ox Home. The advanced practitioner now becomes the illumined sage: *The struggle is over. Gain and loss no longer affect him. He hums the rustic tune of the woodsman and plays the simple songs of the village children. Astride the Ox's back, he gazes serenely at the clouds above.* In the final film of the Japanese classic, Samurai Trilogy, the spiritual warrior prepares for his ultimate duel by becoming a farmer again. Laboring hard in the fields during the day, he carves wooden Buddhas in the evenings by firelight. Eventually he wins his final Samurai encounter, transcending his role as warrior or practitioner, not with a steel but a wooden sword that he carves quickly and surely, drawing on the strength and reverence he developed in the carving of Buddhas. He creates the wooden Buddha and the wooden sword because wood grows directly from the earth. This earthiness of the sage does not mean that he or she is always rural, or rustic. The symbolism here is simplicity, naturalness, spontaneity. The sage, having untethered his own being and the being of all phenomena, begins to blend with the ordinary flow of life. He is pictured sitting comfortably on the Ox: *Riding free as air, he buoyantly comes home through evening mists in wide straw hat and cape. Wherever he may go, he creates a fresh breeze, while in his heart profound tranquillity prevails.* The sage begins spontaneously to radiate Enlightenment, which is no longer simply an insight alive privately within him but a breeze of blessing felt by all who come into his presence. Yet while there is no longer any problem of discovering, catching, or taming the Ox of True Nature, this phase still involves subtle illusion. The sage is still relating to the Ox as a separate being, even though this being is now so intimate that one can ride it effortlessly, without having to pay the slightest attention to where it is going. The Ox must disappear utterly as a separate entity. The Ox must be expressed fully through our own person.

The seventh Ox-herding picture is called Ox Forgotten, Self Alone. The sage finally regards himself as the full expression of True Nature: *There is no twoness. The Ox is his Primal Nature: this he has now recognized. . . . Only on the Ox was he able to come Home. But lo! the Ox has now vanished, and alone and serene sits the man. . . . Yonder, beneath the thatched roof, his idle whip and idle rope are lying.* All spiritual practices and concepts are now idle. There is no longer any question of having to attain or to discipline. The contemplative way has become indistinguishable from daily life. Meditation, nothing more special than walking or breathing, has become the natural activity of the sage and no longer implies any sense of separation or motivation. *Only on the Ox was he able to come Home.* That lingering twoness between the practitioner and his or her True Nature was necessary all along the way until this stage of Coming Home. A new image emerges here. The Ox symbolized True Nature during the period of illusory quest, discipline, and attainment, but the image of Home no longer contains these illusions. Yet although the separate Ox has disappeared, the Enlightened sage himself still exists as a particular embodiment of True Nature. He enjoys serenity and solitude. This subtle twoness created by the separate existence of the sage himself is yet to be dissolved into the perfect singleness of Original Mind. As the roles of seeker and practitioner gradually disappeared, so also the role of sage must cease to limit illumination.

The eighth Ox-herding picture is called Both Ox and Self

1. SEEKING THE OX   The Ox has really never gone astray. Our True Nature is never lost and therefore can never be found.

2. FINDING THE TRACKS   These tracks are the wisdom teaching that all phenomena are the light of Original Mind. Just as differently shaped golden vessels are all basically the same gold, so each and every thing is a manifestation of the Self.

3. FIRST GLIMPSE OF THE OX   This encounter with the Ox does not
come through hearing esoteric teaching but through direct experience. No longer is the Ox imagined to be somewhere out in the
jungle.

4. CATCHING THE OX We must now hold and embrace the Ox, sustain our perception of True Nature with such disciplines as total compassion, perfect nonviolence, unwavering truthfulness.

71

5. TAMING THE OX   An effortless intimacy or friendship with the Ox is being established. The Ox becomes a free companion, not a tool for plowing the field of Enlightenment.

6. RIDING THE OX HOME   The advanced practitioner now becomes the illumined sage. The struggle is over. The sage begins spontaneously to radiate Enlightenment.

7. OX FORGOTTEN, SELF ALONE   The sage finally regards himself as the full expression of True Nature. All spiritual practices and concepts are idle. The contemplative way has become indistinguishable from daily life.

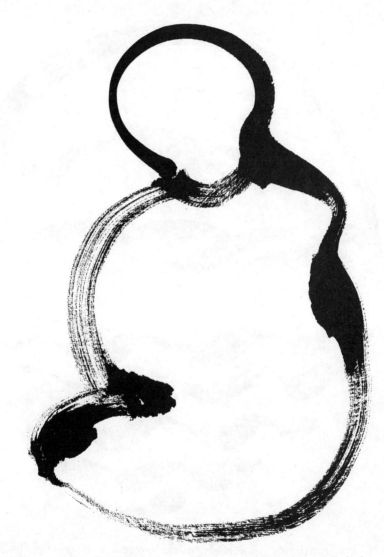

8. BOTH OX AND SELF FORGOTTEN   There is only awakened Enlightenment: no contemplator and no contemplation, no serenity and no disturbance. There is no one, not even the sage.

75

9. RETURN TO THE SOURCE   Formless awareness is growing back into forms again without losing its formless, or perfectly unitary, nature. Enlightenment simply *is* the blue lake and the green mountain.

10. **ENTERING THE MARKETPLACE WITH HELPING HANDS** The cheerful one who fully manifests Enlightenment follows no path. He carries a wine gourd, symbol of the Tantric ecstasy which transforms the wine of the delusive human world from poison into nectar.

Forgotten. The final illusory barrier has evaporated: *All delusive feelings have perished, and ideas of holiness, too, have vanished.* The sage of the previous level has no personal sense of his own holiness but does entertain a sense of reverence for True Nature as expressed through his own conscious being. Instead of blending completely with True Nature, he remains in a contemplative mood and experiences a bliss that still retains a trace of twoness. But on the eighth level, represented by empty space, there is only awakened Enlightenment: no contemplator and no contemplation, no serenity and no disturbance. *He lingers not in Buddha and passes quickly on through not-Buddha.* Awakened Enlightenment itself cannot assert *I am Buddha*, any more than it can assert, *I am not Buddha*. Any such assertion implies the existence of someone who frames the assertion. Here there is no one, not even the sage. Both Ox and Self Forgotten is represented by the traditional Zen circle, the single brushstroke leaving the paper shortly before the point of closure. If there were not that opening, further growth could not occur and the process of Enlightenment would be frozen into empty space. This profound state of emptiness needs to open into fullness. Otherwise it would be excluding the flow of life outside itself, and another illusory sense of subtle duality would arise. The empty circle should contain a landscape. The stream of life-forms continues to flow as trees, fish, insects. Life is not to be locked out by Enlightenment.

The ninth Ox-herding picture is called Return to the Source. Mountains and pine groves, clouds and waves are appearing from nowhere. The open space of emptiness is melting into a kind of springtime: formless awareness is growing back into forms again without losing its formless, or perfectly unitary, nature. The Enlightened being is no longer faced with the illusion of Enlightenment: *From the very beginning there has not been so much as a speck of dust to mar the intrinsic purity.* After the First Glimpse of the Ox, the practitioner senses every activity as emerging directly from the Source, yet must traverse all the subtle intervening levels of development in order actually to return to that Source. The sage's homecoming had to dissolve into the circle of emptiness before he could completely disappear and simply *be* the Source. But there is no annihilation. All manifestation is now observed by awakened Enlightenment as its own emanation: *This waxing and waning of life is no phantom or illusion but a manifestation of the Source. Why, then, is there a need to strive for anything? The waters are blue, the mountains are green.* Enlightenment simply *is* the blue lake and the green mountain. In earlier stages there has been a dramatic quality of realization, but in the ninth stage this drama fades, leaving only freshness or plainness: *The waters are blue, the mountains are green.* But where are the human beings? There remains a subtly transhuman flavor in this Return to the Source. The process of Enlightenment has come so far, through so many simplifications, that there is difficulty in recognizing and accepting the constructions of human personality and society: *It is as though he were now blind and deaf. Seated in his hut, he hankers not for things outside.* There is a subtle twoness here between the Source flowering as pine or cherry trees and its manifestation as the chronic delusion and suffering of human civilization. This very Return to the Source must deepen to include the return to mundane life.

The tenth Ox-herding picture, which obliterates oneness as well as twoness, is called Entering the Marketplace with Helping Hands. Awakened Enlightenment takes the form of a fat, jolly rustic who wanders from village to village, from mundane situation to mundane situation. His body is overflowing with life-energy. His being is full of compassionate love. His open hands express perfect emptiness. *The gate of his cottage is closed, and even the wisest cannot find him.* He has gone beyond, gone completely beyond, not to move farther away from humanity but to return completely into the human world. He has even abandoned the Source as a citadel where Enlightenment may subtly isolate itself. *The wisest cannot find him,* because it is not he that wanders about but simply the activity of awakened Enlightenment. He does not experience any intrinsic difference between himself and the villagers, or even the village landscape: *His mental panorama has finally disappeared. He goes his own way, making no attempt to follow the steps of earlier sages.* Advanced practitioners and even sages feel intense reverence for previous sages, and thereby may regard themselves as subtly separate from those Great Ones. But the awakened Enlightenment expressed in this tenth stage is fully identical with the Enlightenment of all Buddhas, past, present, and future. Who is there to follow? The cheerful one who fully manifests Enlightenment follows no path. He carries a wine gourd, symbol of the Tantric ecstasy which transforms the wine of the delusive human world from poison into nectar. *Carrying a gourd, he strolls into the market. He leads innkeepers and fishmongers in the Way of the Buddha. Bare-chested, barefooted, he comes into the marketplace. Muddied amd dust-covered, how broadly he grins! Without recourse to mystic powers, withered trees he swiftly brings to bloom.* By being perceived as intrinsically Buddhas, not only fishmongers and innkeepers but all human beings in the marketplace of desire are swiftly brought to bloom.

To confirm and enrich the traditional description of Enlightenment provided by the ten Ox-herding pictures, we turn to a contemporary Japanese woman who traversed the higher levels of Enlightenment during an intense period of five days and then died at the age of twenty-five. Yaeko was a physically weak young woman, plagued by illness, whose spiritual dedication was extraordinarily powerful. She practiced five years of intensive *zazen,* or meditation on True Nature, while confined to her bed, visited periodically in her home by Zen master Harada Roshi. During those five years of patient practice she traversed the levels of Enlightenment called Seeking the Ox and Finding the Tracks, and eventually arrived at the First Glimpse of the Ox, the sudden and inebriating experience of all phenomena as Original Mind. During the five days following this *kensho,* or glimpse of her True Nature, Yaeko traversed all the remaining levels of Enlightenment, a process of spiritual evolution that ordinarily takes the advanced practitioner an entire lifetime. We will be reading from Yaeko's letters to her Zen master describing her ecstatic experience and growth of insight during these miraculous five days. The statements of Harada Roshi, confirming Yaeko's growth from his own perspective of Entering the Marketplace with Helping Hands, are remarks he jotted in the margins of her letters.

Yaeko writes: *Yesterday morning you told me, "What you have perceived is still hazy." So I felt I must search more deeply. When I awoke suddenly last midnight, it had become far clearer. . . . All I could do was raise my hands, palms together, out of joy, sheer joy. Truly I see that there are degrees of depth in Enlightenment.* Harada Roshi comments: *Yes, but few know of this significant fact. . . . The Ox has come a hundred miles nearer.* The hazy perception of True Nature referred to here was Yaeko's kensho, or First Glimpse of the Ox. She has now entered the greater clarity of the fourth phase, Catching the Ox. Many practitioners, for years after the experience, accept an inebriating glimpse of True Nature or the flash of initial Enlightenment as final. The actual discovery of higher levels of Enlightenment is, as the roshi remarks, rare. From this new perspective Yaeko continues: *I am ashamed of my defects and will make every effort to discipline my character.* She is now an advanced practitioner, enjoying sustained perception of the Ox, and as such is beginning to open to the task of disciplining her character. She realizes that the direct experience of all phenomena as Original Mind is the beginning of spiritual discipline rather than the sudden release from responsibility that the egocentric seeker may imagine Enlightenment to be. The discipline implied in Catching the Ox does not involve the strict practices and doctrinal concepts used by a seeker or beginning practitioner. It is a refining and expanding process carried on without ambition or striving.

The fragmentation or imperfections that even the advanced spiritual practitioner projects onto True Nature, and which Yaeko calls her *defects*, are perceived clearly in this dimension of Enlightenment. From the more comprehensive standpoint of the sage, however, such perceptions are illusory. The sage sees nothing other than the expanse of True Nature and therefore understands that there are no imperfections. Remarks Harada Roshi: *You have seen the Ox clearly, but the point of grasping it is ten thousand miles away. Your experience is still tinged with conceptual thinking.* This *grasping* of which the roshi speaks is a comprehending or embracing, which refers to the fifth dimension of Enlightenment, Taming the Ox. At that stage all notion of striving—or *conceptual thinking*, as the roshi expresses it—is replaced by intimate friendliness with True Nature in all its manifestations, transcendental and mundane.

Though ten thousand miles away from Home, Yaeko begins to experience a close connection with all other beings. She is able to regard them as expressions of her own True Nature, as a mother sees her children. This connectedness with living beings becomes to the spiritual practitioner primarily the sense of compassion and the intense desire that all beings awaken to their intrinsic Enlightenment. Affirms Yaeko: *Now that my Mind's eye is opened, the vow to save every living being arises in me spontaneously.* The paradox in this vow of compassionate commitment to each being is that, as Enlightenment becomes progressively deeper, it becomes clearer that there are no individual beings separate from True Nature.

As well as all-embracing compassion, Yaeko's experience at this level involves immense personal assurance. She writes: *Even you, Harada Roshi, no longer count for anything in my eyes.* This assurance is not arrogance but the ecstasy that perceives pupil and teacher equally as True Nature. This ecstasy paradoxically includes intense gratitude to the master: . . . *my gratitude and delight are impossible to describe. . . . I write you now only because I think that you alone can understand my happiness, and will be pleased with me.* On the basis of Yaeko's assurance, her compassion, and her dedication to spiritual practice, Harada Roshi confirms that she has not only *glimpsed* but actually *perceives* the Ox: *She has truly seen the Ox, for there is in her experience deep self-affirmation, the desire to save all sentient beings, and the determination to discipline herself spiritually in her daily life.* The roshi notes, however, that even after Yaeko completes the stage of Taming the Ox, there is the long process of Riding the Ox Home: *Only such an exalted state of mind can be called a mind of true children of the Buddha. But as yet there remains a subject who is seeing. Her mind's home is still far distant.*

Yaeko's second letter expresses a remarkable deepening of Enlightenment. She has traversed Taming the Ox and Riding the Ox Home and has arrived at Ox Forgotten, Self Alone, where she is no longer the advanced practitioner but the illumined sage. Yaeko's evolution, which would ordinarily take years of further practice and guidance after the level of Enlightenment indicated in her first letter, has been miraculously condensed into a single day. Writes Yaeko: *Today for the first time I have attained Great Enlightenment. I am so overjoyed that all of me is dancing.* A clue to the depth of this experience is the phrase *all of me.* Nothing is excluded. Her entire being, transcendental and mundane, is perceived as True Nature. Harada Roshi remarks: *Now, for the first time, you have found the way—fully realized your Mind. You have been delivered from delusion, which has no abiding root. Wonderful! Wonderful!* Yaeko continues: *No one but you can possibly understand such ecstasy . . . there is absolutely no delusion. There is neither Ox nor man . . . I have seen my face before my parents were born, clearer than a diamond in the palm of my hand. No longer have I need for dokusan, and all the koan are now like useless furniture to me.* This last phrase contains an element of high-level illusion, as Harada Roshi later comments. Yaeko will have much further need for dokusan, or spiritual guidance, although the koan, or Zen puzzles, are indeed useless to her now as she clearly perceives all phenomena to be her Original Mind.

One of the deceptions that arise again and again during the long process of Enlightenment is the premature rejection of spiritual instruction and guidance. For the advanced practitioner, this deception does not stem from ordinary egotism but from unassimilated ecstasy, which confers an illusory finality on the level of Enlightenment he or she has reached. However, Yaeko's Great Enlightenment, though not final, is certainly far clearer than kensho, or the first glimpse of True Nature. As Yaeko writes: *Those who have only kensho do not know this state of unlimited freedom and profound peace of mind. Indeed it cannot be known until one comes to full enlightenment. If after reading this letter you still talk nonsense to me, I will not hesitate to say your own realization is lacking.* The term *nonsense* is used by practitioners of Zen to describe some spiritual concept, such as goal-oriented practice or gradual purification, that implies any obscuration of True Nature. Such nonsense, or illusion of twoness, is an unavoidable aspect of each stage of Enlightenment, and the nonsensical concept of Enlightenment itself still remains with Yaeko. Harada Roshi exclaims: *Good! Good! This is called the stage of standing on a summit of a lone mountain, or coming back to one's own Home. Yet I have to talk nonsense to you. You will understand why someday.*

Yaeko has plunged so deeply into ecstasy that she is able playfully to threaten her Zen master, to call his realization into question. She perceives herself as a fully realized master, or sage: *When I reflect that I have actually fulfilled the Great Vow made by me through numberless past lives and can now hold dokusan, I am infinitely grateful.* Yaeko later comes to regard these remarks as the result of unassimilated ecstasy and withdraws her premature claim to being a roshi who can offer others dokusan, or spiritual guidance to Enlightenment. Concerning Yaeko's claim to have transcended discipleship, Harada Roshi remarks: *It is too early yet. Still, how many among those called enlightened have established such inner assurance?* For Yaeko there is no longer any need to realize True Nature or to deepen this realization, for such projects are now perceived as *nonsense*. There is only the sense of assurance that her entire being is already True Nature. Yaeko's assurance is recognized by her illumined guide as confirmation that she has actually come Home. As Yaeko exclaims: *Neither Buddhas nor devils can unnerve me. This stage defies description. I have forgotten everything and returned to my real Home empty-handed.*

Although she has come Home into the empty, radiant expanse of Original Mind, Yaeko's compassionate commitment to all beings intensifies. And although she no longer needs any spiritual discipline or special practice, her desire for deeper and deeper clarity expresses itself spontaneously through every thought and perception of daily life. *Now I can commence the unending task of rescuing every living being. This makes me so happy I can scarcely contain myself. All is radiance, pure radiance. I can now forever progress toward perfection in natural harmony with my daily life.* In the light of these words, *forever progress toward perfection,* the ten Ox-herding pictures themselves become *nonsense,* because the dimensions of Enlightenment are perceived to be endless, traversed and retraversed, in various moods, eternally. Harada Roshi joyfully responds: *You do comprehend. That is exactly how it is. How many so-called Zen men these days have come to such profound realization? . . . I am so thankful to have a disciple like you that I can now die happily.* That the process of Enlightenment is eternal is further suggested by Yaeko, who writes: *I have been resurrected, as have you and everything else, for all eternity.* The Buddhist view teaches, from the standpoint of the seeker, that all phenomena continuously change, and yet Yaeko suggests, from the standpoint of the sage, that she and all phenomena have been resurrected for eternity. She is here revealing that Enlightenment is timeless, not linked to the arising and passing away of single moments or entire civilizations but shining through all and irradiating all phenomena with a sense of eternal presence.

Yaeko continues: *You alone can understand my mind. Yet there is neither you nor me. My body and mind in fact have completely dropped away.* When the person unattuned to Original Mind looks at body, mind, and world, these appear opaque, or solid, and he or she encounters apparent separation and fragmentation. To the sage, by contrast, all structure is revealed as transparent, in no way obscuring the flow of True Nature. Thus Yaeko continues to write and convey gratitude to Harada Roshi, even though she perceives him and herself as perfectly transparent to True Nature. Yaeko exclaims: *I am in the center of the Great Way, where everything is natural, without strain, neither hurried nor halting; where there are no Buddhas, no you, nothing; and where I see without my eyes and hear without my ears. Not a trace remains of what I have written. There is neither pen nor paper nor words—nothing at all.* Yaeko here authentically expresses her Enlightenment. After she writes this ecstatic letter, the words and concepts are seen by her to disappear immediately into the expanse of Original Mind. The roshi remarks: *This degree of illumination is . . . the true attainment of the Way. It is the return to one's own Home.*

Her next letter indicates that Yaeko has already assimilated the ecstasy of Great Enlightenment. Writes Yaeko: *My letter of the twenty-fifth must have led you to think that I had gone mad . . . I had reached such a peak of ecstasy that I couldn't contain myself. When I recovered my senses . . . I burst into laughter at the thought of how topsy-turvy my emotions had become.* The roshi responds: *You need not rebuke yourself. The delirium of joy is the initial reaction of all who have had a deep awakening.* This delirium is experienced during the sixth phase of Enlightenment, Riding Home on the Ox of True Nature, drunk with subtle ecstasy. Because it contrasts so dramatically with ordinary, daily experience, this ecstasy helps to sustain the illusory separation between spiritual life and ordinary life. These two categories of experience must disappear into each other so completely that, in a sense, neither remains. Yaeko continues from her new level of clarity or maturity: *I am profoundly aware of the need for diligent self-cultivation and thoroughly understand the value of dokusan. I swear never again to write anything so pretentious as I did yesterday, saying that I had become enlightened and therefore could instruct others in do-*

kusan. To this refusal by Yaeko to claim Enlightenment, the roshi responds simply and powerfully, *You have truly awakened.* He goes on to remark: *Though it takes five to ten years after kensho for most devotees to come to this stage, she has reached it in less than a week.* Yaeko has entered the phase of Both Ox and Self Forgotten, which involves the disappearance of the illusion that Enlightenment is a condition one can claim. Subtle pretensions are dissipated, and even the role of illumined sage is transcended.

In the fourth letter of Yaeko to Harada Roshi, this remarkable acceleration continues: *Forgive me for writing you so often. I have attained the level of realization which is the last possible while yet a disciple.* Yaeko's balanced assimilation of ecstasy is now such that new levels of Enlightenment do not disturb her appreciation of discipleship. The roshi, observing her selfless assurance, responds simply: *Indeed you have.* Yaeko proceeds to describe the ordinariness of Return to the Source, the ninth phase of Enlightenment. *I used to think, "How grand one must become upon enlightenment," and "How admirable is he who devotes himself so fully to Buddhist activities, that he no longer thinks of himself." But I was so mistaken!* Yaeko understands that, although Enlightened, she is an ordinary human being. The pure Buddha activity which is now consciously focused through her is simply her full humanity. There is nothing particularly sublime about it. *Before enlightenment I was so anxious for it, and often thought, "How noble is he who returns Home with peace and contentment." But having come to full enlightenment, I now say to myself, "Why were you so excited about it?" For I have a distinct aversion to being called "enlightened."* The illumined sage has disappeared into the Source, leaving only a transcendent flash of humor, as Yaeko writes: *It tickles me to say to myself, "So this is full enlightenment!"*

We have seen three kinds of transcendent emotion radiating from Enlightenment: compassion, gratitude, and now laughter. Each is without object or subject and is marked by spontaneity. Although she has disappeared into the Source, Yaeko continues to express gratitude: *I can't tell you how thankful I am to be forever one with the true Dharma, utterly and naturally.* No longer is there any question of further practice and purification, as in previous letters, but a sense of effortless oneness with Dharma, or True Nature. Harada Roshi characterizes Yaeko's level of realization as *that condition of absolute naturalness where the mutual interpenetration of the world of discrimination and the world of equality is so thorough that one is consciously aware of neither.* Having disappeared into the Source, there is neither the fragmenting ignorance of discrimination nor the unifying wisdom that perceives the equality of all phenomena. In the center of the sun, there is neither night nor day. As Yaeko exclaimed in an earlier letter, *I am in the center of the Great Way. . . . All is radiance, pure radiance.*

Yet now not only the ecstasy but the insight itself has disappeared into the Source. Yaeko writes: *I have utterly forgotten the moment of my enlightenment. . . . I simply can't understand why I always made such a to-do about respecting Buddhism or anyone who had attained full enlightenment.* Harada Roshi comments on Yaeko's present level of Enlightenment-beyond-Enlightenment: *One who has attained to this degree has completed what Zen practice can be carried out under a teacher and embarked upon the path of true self-practice.* Yaeko, no longer asserting independence from her teacher, has really become her own roshi, or master. Better, Original Mind has become the guide.

Although there is no separate Buddha, intense reverence and gratitude flow toward the being who transmits this understanding. Writes Yaeko: *Thanks to you, I have clearly perceived that the Buddha is none other than Mind. My gratitude knows no bounds. This is as much due to your benevolent guidance as to my intense longing and striving for Buddhahood that I may save all living beings.* The roshi responds: *I had not thought of you as one with such an unusually strong aspiration toward Bud-*

dhahood. How undiscerning of me! It is evident that you are the incarnation of a great Bodhisattva.

At this point it becomes clear to the roshi that Yaeko is drawing on previous lifetimes of spiritual practice and that she is headed beyond the various levels of Enlightenment to Buddhahood, the dawning of which is glimpsed in the tenth, and last, Ox-herding picture. Buddhahood is a flow of ultimate power. The compassionate vow to save all living beings can be fulfilled gradually, moment by moment or lifetime by lifetime, by the Bodhisattva, or being who is traversing the various levels of Enlightenment. But this vow can be fulfilled instantaneously by a Buddha, who sees all beings as already Buddhas. *All beings are already saved,* affirms the living Buddha. The actual spiritual power released by this affirmation subtly permeates the awareness of all beings and tangibly intensifies their evolutionary energy. This affirmation, which is Buddhahood, is already the True Nature of each living being. As Yaeko, or Harada before her, enters conscious Buddhahood, this beginningless affirmation of True Nature is once again confirmed. Yaeko has Entered the Marketplace with Helping Hands. The affirmation of True Nature radiates from her spontaneously, bringing countless seekers and practitioners to bloom. At this very moment we are being touched directly by her transmission.

For Yaeko at the culmination of Enlightenment there no longer appears any aspirant teacher, or transmission. As she reveals to Harada Roshi, all levels of Enlightenment have disappeared into *tada.* Tada means literally in Japanese *only,* or *just.* As the Zen master advises us: *When you eat, just eat. When you walk, only walk.* Tada is perfect transparency expressed through dailiness. Tada is *just* Buddhahood, *only* True Nature. There is nothing else. Writes Yaeko: *The further I advance on the Supreme Way, the more exalted it becomes. I have experienced that tada itself is perfection.* All sense of doing is left behind in tada, and yet no detail of any heavenly or earthly sphere is ignored by tada, which is caring and careful. As

Yaeko writes, *I promise myself to act with the utmost care in every detail of my life.* Not only is every sentient being Buddha, every detail is Buddha.

Two days after fully realizing herself to be Buddha, Yaeko died. She disappeared entirely into tada. To tada alone can we offer our profound gratitude.

I am in the center of the Great Way, where everything is natural, without strain, neither hurried nor halting. I can't tell you how thankful I am to be forever one with the true Dharma, utterly and naturally. It tickles me to say to myself, "So this is full enlightenment!" —Yaeko

CHAPTER FIVE

THERE IS ONLY THE ONE

Plotinus and the Metaphysics of
(3rd Century *Spiritual Quest*

B.C.

Plotinus, who lived during the third century, writes what may be the most coherent spiritual metaphysics in Western or Eastern tradition. What we encounter in Plotinus and his teacher, Ammonius Saccas, is a stream of high wisdom and contemplative practice that flows through the ancient Pythagoreans, through Socrates and later Greek culture, and into European mystical thought. Heidegger, for instance, reflects clearly the intellectual and spiritual transmission of Plotinus, the Neoplatonic lineage that has been sustained by the Christian mystics and transcendental Western philosophers.

Aspects of the spiritual quest and the nature of Ultimate Reality were questions that Plato touched but Plotinus developed thoroughly, although the writings of Plotinus are not a philosophical system but a loose collection of discourses based on conversations with various students of philosophy. Plotinus was not merely an independent thinker, engaging in his own personal speculations, but a disciplined initiate into the contemplative tradition embodied by his teacher, Ammonius. Having traveled to Alexandria in search of an authentic teacher of philosophy who could serve as a spiritual guide while maintaining the highest intellectual standards, Plotinus, at the age of twenty-seven, encountered Ammonius. This enigmatic person, like Socrates, wrote nothing, but embodied, in his own spiritual realization, the esoteric interpretation of Plato's thought which had blossomed in Alexandria among the various wisdom teachings of Jewish, Christian, and Greek Gnosticism. Although there was access in Alexandria to Indian culture, through trade that was occurring between Egypt and the Far East, Neoplatonism appears to have developed, quite independent of Indian spirituality, as a mystical flowering of the Greek Way.

The moment Plotinus encountered Ammonius, he knew this was the person he had been searching for among various philosophical circles. There was more to Ammonius than brilliance. The power of realization radiated from him directly to his student Plotinus. Concerning Ultimate Reality and how the student comes to know It, Plato writes in his Seventh Epistle: *I certainly have composed no work in regard to It, for there is no way of putting It in words like other studies. Acquaintance with It must come after a long period of instruction and companionship, when suddenly, like a blaze kindled by a leaping spark, It is generated in the soul, and the mind is flooded with light.*

We will be exploring primarily this question of Ultimate Reality, which Plotinus terms the One, but will refer as well to some of his rich insights into the structure of the relative dimension, which he regards as the eternal procession of Being from the One. Since Plotinus never philosophized systematically but approached the One in various moods and from various directions, we will follow the free association of his thought rather than organize the sparks of his insight into any strict form.

For Plotinus, the One is not an abstraction, nor an empty or static Absolute. The One is that Power, utterly simple yet rich in potentiality, that generates Being and the various planes of Being—not physically or psychically but more as a mathematical principle generates a series of numbers. Unlike a mathematical formula, however, the One is a living principle and the infinite series of beings It entails are radiantly alive. Nor is Being one-dimensional, like a mathematical series, but is an emanation of beings simultaneously on several distinct planes of existence, each of which expresses in a different metaphysical key the single potency of the One. The One is more alive, for instance, than the life-energy of organic beings, which are Its emanations on a less primal plane of existence. Plotinus also refers to the One as the Good, the ground of all human concern for value, yet for Plotinus the One can never be an object of rational thought. The One is not a philosophical category but a spiritual reality that Plotinus directly realized as the intrinsic nature of all beings and all planes of Being.

Plotinus speaks of the One as Love, although the One possesses no personhood. The One is not the personal God, whom Plotinus describes with reverence as the Cosmic Soul, an emanation of the One on a more primal level of Being than the physical universe. The One is utterly primary— more primary, even, than Being itself. Because of this primacy, we cannot make any literal assertion about the One. Plotinus cautions, *Speaking of the One, "as it were" must be understood with every term.* The *via negativa*, which asserts nothing positive about the Divine but only what the Divine is not, was introduced into Western mystical theology from Plotinus. Although Plotinus often attempts to reveal positive glimpses of the One through suggestion rather than assertion, in the mood of via negativa he remarks: *Every inquiry is either about what a thing essentially is, or its quality, or its cause, or the fact of its existence, but none of this applies to the One.* Plotinus proceeds so far along the via negativa as to call the One *that which does not exist.* The One is too simple, too ultimate, too primal to express any condition of existence or to possess any quality, although existence and all its qualities emanate from the One. The One is not caused by any force, not even by Itself, because It does not exist in the forceful, substantial way in which we experience existence. The One is impossible to objectify, because it is radically simple—simpler, even, than unity. Teaches Plotinus: *We can call It "One" if we remember that It is not something that possesses the attribute of unity.*

The One is not even one. How should we proceed in the face of such an impasse? Plotinus responds: *We should make no inquiry about It but simply touch It in our intellect and learn that it is a profanation to apply any terms to It.* Plotinus regards intellect, termed *nous* in Greek, not as the step-by-step process of ordinary thinking or rational inquiry but as the permanently illumined dimension of human awareness which allows for immediate intuition. *Nous* is the mysterious mode of knowing that envisions wholes rather than investigating parts, and therefore it is through the illumined intellect that we touch the One, which is the principle of all wholeness. Language need not disappear entirely in this dimension of intellectual vision. *Profanation in applying terms to It* exists only if we imagine these terms to be literal or binding. For Plotinus, intellectual vision resembles the Zen experience of sudden Enlightenment which penetrates immediately to the intrinsic nature of consciousness, *touching* it rather than thinking about it. Yet this is a subtle and arduous process in both Zen and Plotinian ways of wisdom.

Plotinus undercuts any approach to the One based on ordinary thinking, which always tends to separate us from the Ultimate. Writes Plotinus: *We investigate Its presence and Its existence as if It were a stranger, projected into our imaginary "place" from some depth or height.* We may imagine that the One, since It is absolute, must be distant from us spiritually or even spatially—that we must bridge some impassable gulf to touch the One or that the One must *descend* into our mind to reveal Itself. We forget that the absoluteness of the One includes absolute immanence, or omnipresence. Thus the One is here and now, not a stranger, not even an *other*, but the very nature of what we are. And Plotinus speaks of mundane existence as our *imaginary place*, because we are not fundamentally situated in space any more than the One is. We do not really have a *place*, because we are essentially nothing but the One overflowing Itself into experience.

Plotinus teaches that the One overflows spontaneously and eternally as several planes or levels of Being. He uses the verbs *overflow, emanate,* and *proceed* for this timeless process which is metaphysical rather than physical. The most primary, or highest level of Being is the Realm of Intellectual Vision. At this level there is no physical universe, nor are there even heavenly realms. There exist only the vibrant almost musical seeds from which souls and eventually organic beings proceed on less primal planes of Being. These Archetypes interpenetrate harmoniously, free from the structure of space and time. The musical quality of this metaphysical realm springs from its intrinsic activity of praising the One. As Plotinus explains, all emanations of the One by nature turn to contemplate or praise their Source.

Since the One is boundless power, this overflow continues into a second and lower plane of Being, the Realm of Soul. There is still no physical universe but there now appear individual souls, living in communion, sharing transcendental or heavenly life in eternal contemplation of the One. The overflow continues and finally begins to dissipate into the shadow of Being which is nonbeing. Here the physical universe and its life-forms take shape as the intersection, as it were, of Being and nonbeing. This is the third emanation of the One, the Realm of life. The conscious beings that naturally evolve in the tangible universe are rays from the Realm of Soul that focus through various biological structures. The Realm of Soul encompasses the Realm of Life, and therefore organic life does not exist *outside* Soul.

The procession of Being may be imagined as movement outward from a center, like the growth rings of a tree. But this metaphysical procession is more accurately understood as an emanation inward toward the disappearing point of pure nonbeing. In this way, the One is seen to encompass Its emanations. The physical universe is the most restricted emanation of the One, and closest as it were, to nonbeing. Nonetheless, organic life is still an emanation of the One, and physical life-forms turn naturally to contemplate their Source. This *turning* is expressed through the evolution of all sentient beings and through what human beings experience as the mystical quest.

When Plotinus speaks of our souls, he refers to the Realm of Soul, not to some location within the body or the universe. Writes Plotinus: *Soul is not "in" the universe, but the universe is "in" it: body is not a "place" for Soul.* Similarly, the One is not *in* any being or phenomenon, but all phenomena are *in* the One, or Ultimate Consciousness. Modern scientific myth, by contrast, imagines that consciousness is a product of enigmatic physical evolution. Massive clouds of energy condense into galaxies, our scientists assert, and from chemical reactions there develop molecular seeds that eventually evolve consciousness as animals and human beings. Plotinus would suggest that such a view is the opposite of what is actually the case. Not physical energy but Consciousness is the primary reality, the One. Within the One, though not in any spatial sense, evolve various planes of Being. On the most limited of these planes appear the swirling clouds of galactic energy that we call the universe, where biological structures evolve to express the One, or Consciousness. To glimpse this insight, there must be a shift in our perspective comparable to a figure/ground reversal. Instead of imagining human beings as insignificant points of awareness in the vast physical universe, we must realize that the Consciousness which human beings really *are* is the One, containing galaxies within itself as thoughts are said to be *contained* by the mind.

Plotinus suggests that when the soul becomes embodied, which is the common but inaccurate expression, there is actually no *coming down* from the Realm of Soul, no *contracting* within a particular nervous system, because the soul is not spatial. Plotinus explains that our souls live, now as always, on higher, or more primal, planes of Being. These higher places contain no spatial multiplicity, only the perfectly inter-penetrating, spaceless multiplicity of spiritual Archetypes, which provide unique principles for each soul.

The manifestation of souls on the physical plane may be pictured in this way. Our Archetype, perhaps fertilized by other Archetypes, gives birth to a particular child, or soul-ray, which becomes identified as our present body-mind. The Archetype, as Mother, becomes deeply involved with Her child, perhaps one of many in various galaxies. But when the child evolves and begins to realize the full extent of its nature as the One, the Mother, or Archetype, returns to Her universal Life, in which the particular soul now fully partici-pates. The Enlightened human being thus develops an awareness on the level of his or her Archetype, which is sometimes regarded as a Divine Form. Many humans are still young children, almost entirely unaware of levels of Being more primal than their particular body-mind.

As our soul contemplates its Archetype, so that Archetype in turn contemplates the One, which is its Source. Plotinus always returns to the One as the intrinsic nature of the entire procession of Being. The body-mind is in the soul, the soul is in the Archetype, the Archetype is in the One, but the One is not situated in a more comprehensive reality. Explains Plotinus: *The One is in nothing at all, and therefore in this sense "nowhere."* . . . *It is therefore not far from anything, although not in anything.* The One is situated nowhere, and for this reason cannot be separated from us by the slightest physical or psychic space. It is utterly close and accessible.

The One, although not characterized by substance or by existence, expresses boundless power, not physical or psychic power but the metaphysical fruitfulness of ever-expanding implications or horizons. Writes Plotinus: *The One must be considered infinite not by unlimited extensions of size or number but by the unboundedness of Its power.* The cosmic process through which energy and eventually matter are created is the small-est fiber of the One's generative power. But this power has no object, no direction. As Plotinus explains: *The One, perfect because It seeks nothing, needs nothing, overflows, as it were, and Its superabundance makes something, as it were, other than Itself, which is Being.* This overflow of the One is intrinsically nothing but the One. Nor is the One in any way aware of having overflowed and generated what we call Being. Plotinus, however, does not develop the Indian notion of *maya*, the sense that manifest Being is somehow illusory. He may consider that there is illusion involved in the separation of beings in the space-time realm, which is the intersection of Being and nonbeing, but the primal realms of Being, where archetypal structures interpenetrate spacelessly and timelessly, are for Plotinus completely real. These realms are as real as the One, for they *are* the One. The realms of Being, which are the One as It eternally overflows, can never be withdrawn, because the One is superabundance of Power. Although the One thus inevitably emanates as Being, It cannot be defined in terms of Being, nor can It be limited to Being. Nonetheless, beings are not separate from the One, which is their own beinghood. As Plotinus remarks: . . . *it is by the One that all beings are beings.*

Thinking pursues the multiplication of possibilities, whereas the intellectual vision of Plotinus moves in the direction of simplicity. The One is utmost simplicity. Writes Plotinus: *The One is not thinking, for there is no otherness in It. It does not think Itself.* Possibility exists only for thinking. There are no possibilities for the One. Even the notion of infinite possibilities is a limiting concept in the light of the One, which does not think about Itself, much less about possibilities. Plotinus remarks about this absence for the One of any relation to Itself: *We ought not, in fact, even speak of "self-presence."* The One is not aware of Itself but is primal awareness itself. The One cannot be present to Itself in any way, for there is nothing for It to reflect on or to reflect against. The realms of Being are not experienced by the One as other than Itself. Otherness, or separation from the One, is only experienced by beings such as ourselves, who are manifest in the realm of physical energy, where, because of the interplay of Being and nonbeing, the illusion of separation arises. Plotinus continues: *We ought not to class the One as a "thinking being" but, rather, simply as "awareness," for awareness does not think.* The One, or primal awareness, is not a process of articulating, not consciousness-of but Consciousness without any object or subject. We cannot apply to the One any conventional ideas about awareness, for our relative awareness functions as consciousness-of. But we should remember that this primal simplicity of Ultimate Consciousness is not in some way sterile, or barren. The One is the richness that becomes articulated in our relative awareness as thinking and loving.

Plotinus always speaks of the One figuratively, for, as he reminds us, nothing whatsoever can be attributed to the One. The figurative language of Plotinus often contrasts or even clashes from discourse to discourse. This should not surprise us, because Plotinus was describing a Reality that he knew could not be described. The language of Plotinus, however, has the power to awaken the intellectual vision that *touches* the One—in other words, the primal awareness that *is* the One. Exercising this free play of figurative language, Plotinus occasionally describes our turning or awakening to the One through the metaphor of the One noticing Itself, though no self-awareness in any ordinary sense is implied. He writes: *The One has only a kind of simple intuition directed to Itself. But since It is in no way distant or different from Itself, what can this intuitive regard of Itself be other than Itself?* Ramana Maharshi teaches us to inquire, *Who am I?* We never receive an answer to that inquiry but simply stop questioning. Why do we stop? Because we realize that, in Plotinus' terms, *the intuitive regard of Itself is Itself.* This intuitive regard, or the *Who am I?*, is none other than the Ultimate Consciousness we are seeking along the way of wisdom. This is not, however, like revealing the answer to a puzzle or riddle. These words are mere ciphers until we experience that flash of illumination in which questioning opens into the flower of infinite affirmation.

The One's *intuitive regard of Itself* is Its own overflow as Being, the very nature of which is the questioning or questing that we eventually perceive as the mystical path. Plotinus elucidates: *The One is born, so to speak, to Its own interior as if in love of the clear light which is Itself, and It is what It loves.* We sense the sublimity of love in our human experience because the One loves as It overflows, although Its love is free from the distraction of any separate subject or object and is therefore infinitely more intense than ordinary human love. Through Its love, the One is born to Its own interior. We may still cling to the notion that the Divine projects creation *outside* Itself, but the actual case is hinted at by the mystical language of Kabbalah, which suggests that a sliver of negative space, or nonbeing, opens mysteriously within Divine Plenitude in order that there be room, as it were, for the manifest universe to take shape deep within the Divine. Yet all forms that manifest within the One are only, in the words of Plotinus, *the clear light which is Itself.* There is only the One.

The One is not regarded by Plotinus as static, or at rest. The One is the intense activity of superabundant power which emanates as Being. But we must not confuse this activity of the One with the play of physical energy. Suggests Plotinus: *This activity is a kind of awakening, the wakener being no other than Itself; an eternal wakening of super-intellection; the One is as It wakes Itself to be: the wakening is beyond being, beyond essence and beyond conscious life.* Although It is the eternal awakeness beyond Being, the One is not separate. Remarks Plotinus: *It has life in Itself and all things in Itself.* Attempting to explain the nature of the One's absolute activity, Plotinus declares, *The One is an activity, and yet It has no function.* Whereas the idea of function is the central focus of ordinary human thinking and acting, the One is functionless. The overflow of the One as Being has no function or purpose. Buddhist mystics regard the Void as limitlessly creative because its very emptiness or purposelessness imposes no obstruction to manifestation. In a similar vein, Plotinus remarks about the One: *It is because there is nothing in It, that all things come from It; It is the power which begets things while remaining in Itself without undergoing any diminution.* The One possesses no substance, and this is Its perfect fullness, which cannot be diminished.

The One has no investment in any manifestation. As Plotinus explains: *A principle has no need of what comes after It, and the principle of all things needs none of them.* From the principle of a mathematical series, we can generate numbers indefinitely. But the principle does not *need* to generate any of these numbers, although it contains them implicitly. All beings are uniquely vibrating numbers contained by the One as by a living mathematical principle. But the mathematical principle does not *cause* the instances that illustrate it. Remarks Plotinus: *Even when we call the One the Cause, we are not predicating any attribute of It but of ourselves, because we receive something from It while It exists in Itself.* The One does not have any experience of causing us, yet from our standpoint as individual instances of the One, we instinctively but inappropriately think of the One's infinite Power as somehow causal. Plotinus continues: *It does not need the things which have come into being from It, but leaves them all alone because It needs none of them and is the same as It was before It brought them into being; It would not have cared if they had not come into being.* Yet the procession of Being is inevitable, given what Plotinus figuratively calls the *generosity* of the One, which we can imagine as a permanent condition of supersaturation. But the superabundant overflow of the One is still simply the One.

At this point, the devotional seeker may complain: *Doesn't God care if I contemplate Him?* Plotinus would answer that the One is not the personal God. The Cosmic Soul is God, and does indeed care that human beings turn consciously to the One. That Divine caring and human turning are the natural way of Being itself. Yet the One remains at the heart of the caring and turning of Being, without Itself caring or turning. As Plotinus subtly suggests: *The One in Its aloneness can neither know nor be ignorant of anything.* The One cannot be aware of our personal concerns but cannot be ignorant of them either, because It *is* they, as It is the entire procession and contemplative return of Being. The radically transcendent nature of the One does not remove It the slightest distance from any phenomenon. As Plotinus explains: *The One is immanent by Its very transcendence.* The One transcends Being itself, but It is not beyond any life or any concern, no matter how microscopic. The One transcends transcendence.

Human beings are, in the language of Plotinus, the One's Love for the Clear Light which It is. Yet there remains the puzzle of apparent human ignorance concerning the One. Plotinus explains: *You do not really go away from It, for It is there; you do not "go" anywhere, but remain present to It yet turn your back on It.* As Ramana Maharshi teaches, Enlightenment is simply to admit that we are already Enlightened, already the One. This involves a revolution in our attitude, a turning around to what we have turned our back on. This turning is as simple and natural as rising to the surface for air after diving into water, yet requires intense spiritual preparation, for we have become disoriented in the dark waters of space and time. As Plotinus remarks: *The One is present only to those who are prepared for It.* Such preparation, for Plotinus, involves years of contemplative thinking about the One, guided and inspired by a teacher who is grounded consciously in the One. This spiritual discipline can be primarily intellectual, in Plotinus' sense of the illumined intellect, and need not be focused through any religious commitment of a devotional nature.

Whether along the way of devotion or of wisdom, however, spiritual preparation involves channeling the basic longing for the One which animates all beings. Plotinus remarks, *Men have forgotten That which from the beginning and now still they want and long for.* We naturally manifest this ultimate longing, for the very nature of our being, as Being, is to turn and contemplate the One. Such contemplation is even now occurring in the guise of our ordinary lives. Explains Plotinus, *The One is present even to those asleep and does not astonish those who at any time see It, because It is always there.* Enlightenment, or awakening as the One, is not an astonishing or startling experience, for the One is always there as the core of all our awareness. In the process of Enlightenment there is indeed a point when we become ecstatic over rediscovering the One, but this excitement eventually disappears as we understand more clearly that the One is fully present through every state of consciousness, transcendental and mundane.

Ecstatic experience is natural to the process of Enlightenment, whether expressed through some devotional mood or through the bliss of mystical knowing. But ecstasy eventually dissolves into primal awareness. Plotinus identifies ecstasy with the love of Beauty. By the spirituality of Greek culture, Beauty is regarded as a liberating Divinity that one worships with the offering of human beauty in order to be lifted into the ecstatic realm of Divine Beauty. Plotinus insists that such ecstasy can only be secondary to Enlightenment, or awakening as the One: *The passionate love of Beauty, when it comes, causes pain, because one must have seen it to desire it. Beauty is shown to be secondary because this passionote love for it is secondary. The more ancient and unperceived desire for the One proclaims that the One Itself is more ancient than and prior to Beauty.* For Plotinus, passionate love for the Divine or blissful contemplation of the Archetypes are secondary because the intoxication and awe they generate suggest separation, or twoness. The One generates no such emotional response. Writes Plotinus: *The One is gently and graciously present to anyone when a person wishes; Beauty brings wonder and shock and pleasure mingled with pain.* Awakening as the One cannot, therefore, be regarded as an ecstatic experience, accessible only in some special state of consciousness, but is an awakening that pervades all states of consciousness equally.

Enlightenment is to awaken as the One rather than to know or see the One in the way a subject experiences an object. This awakening transcends all levels of experience just as, ontologically speaking, the One transcends all levels of Being. The endless varieties of ecstatic experience are still in the realm of Beauty, or Being. However, because *immanent by Its very transcendence*, the One is not *beyond* or *outside* ecstatic experiences. The One, or Ultimate Consciousness, is the ground of all experience. To be conscious that we are Consciousness is not a separate experience.

Yet the preparation for this non-experience is challenging. Because of the utterly primal or simple nature of the One, we must be simple as well. Our perception of complexity must be explored in depth, gradually becoming transparent to the One. Plotinus calls awakening as the One *the flight of the Alone to the Alone*. The Zen master speaks of *red flowers blooming red*. The repetition in each of these mystical utterances expresses the circular nature of the Awakening. This circularity condenses into the primal affirmation *Is is Is*, which in turn disappears into its Source, the One, revealing the entire drama of Being as the One alone.

The way of wisdom followed by Plotinus is not a philosophical system but a powerful path of initiation that actually serves to awaken us as the One. The writings of Plotinus provide inspiration for actual contemplative practice. They are not meant to function as an academic exercise in metaphysical speculation. We are each at present capable, to some degree, of the intellectual vision that Plotinus wishes to kindle.

I will describe here an instance of such vision, an ascent to the One that occurred to me, through spiritual imagination, while meditating with Mother Serena, an eighty-year-old Rosicrucian teacher immersed in the Western esoteric tradition so deeply enriched by the influence of Plotinus. There is a distinct difference in tone between daydreaming and the unexpected appearance of intense spiritual imagery during meditation. Such visions, or spontaneous visualizations, have occurred to me only rarely during some twelve years of contemplative practice. This imagery is an attempt by the mind, functioning beyond voluntary control, to translate direct spiritual perception into recognizable forms and relationships. Plotinus occasionally uses the metaphor of spiritual ascent although, strictly speaking, there is not the slightest distance between us and the One through which we need ascend.

While listening to Mother Serena read names for healing, seated in the chapel where she has meditated daily for over fifty years, I gradually became aware that I was rising higher in consciousness. While ascending, I could still hear Mother Serena praying for the health and peace of the world, and remained even faintly aware of the sound of trucks on the upper West Side of New York City. This spiritual ascension translated itself vividly into the image of an elevator. The elevator was passing various floors, heavenly realms that I could have stopped to explore, but an aspiration to glimpse its ultimate destination kept me on this visionary elevator. Finally the car reached the top floor, its doors opened, and I stepped into a realm of golden light. My body was of the same color and nature as this light. I was not floating, but fully aware of this golden body, which responded just like my ordinary body. I was also aware of walking on some surface. Intuitively, I sensed this was not the top, not yet the ultimate view. Noticing a stairway that circled upward and was lost in the intensity of golden light, I began to climb, realizing that as I ascended, the light became more dense. My awareness of walking on an ordinary surface began to dissolve. My body blended with the light, and soon there was no body, only golden intensity. I was still aware of myself as an individual center of consciousness, although now there was no sense of climbing any farther, because bodily metaphors had become irrelevant. My awareness hung like a kite in the sky. I was at a loss how to proceed but sensed there was more. Then a revelatory voice, at once clear and tender, inquired if I really wished to realize what is Ultimate. I assented.

The next move resembled osmosis through a membrane and occurred spontaneously, without planning or effort. With no sensation of abruptness, there was the other side of the membrane. All was clear. The heavy golden density of Being was gone, dissipated as though one were to move directly from summer humidity to autumn clarity. The golden light had generated a certain excitement or ecstasy, but now there was none—only clear brightness, natural and buoyant. This brightness was so total that there was no room for an *I*; yet even in the absence of a particular *I*, awareness was fully present. This intense, consuming presence or brightness was not substance but simply clarity of awareness. The clarity appeared white, or faintly opaque, because there was nothing to be seen through this clarity that would make it appear transparent. And because there was nothing to be seen, there was no sense of distance or vastness—only a sense of completeness. This primal awareness is what Plotinus calls the One.

After an interval of simple brightness that revealed nothing beyond itself, the question arose, *How long have you been here?* These words, seeming to filter through from another level of consciousness, kindled an immediate sensation of laughter, because it was delightfully apparent that no such concept could be applied. There must be some sequence of events in order to judge any lapse of time, but if nothing whatsoever is happening, there can be no passage of time or even any observer. After another immeasurable interval, a second question arose: *Why would one ever leave this Clear Light?* As if in response to the query, a bubble appeared, floating through the brightness, resembling the bubbles children blow from rings dipped in soap. When sunlight shines through these soap bubbles, rainbow colors appear. Just so, within this bubble there stretched a rainbow, which revealed itself as the entire structure of Being—all the planes, all the souls, all the sentient beings, civilizations, and galaxies. The whole structure was totally insubstantial. The bubble, unstable as it floated, changed shape constantly, looking as if it might burst at any moment. Its delicacy was poignant. And the seamless brightness of the One shone directly through this transparent bubble of Being. Then a current of loving concern welled up, concern for the beings on these various planets and planes of rainbow light. That concern became more and more intense, building to a climax. Suddenly I found myself once more in the golden realm, understanding that I had been taken back through the membrane into this floating bubble which is Being.

My sense of individuality reawakened as soon as I perceived the golden light. Yet I knew that I had been returned to Being not by attachment to my individuality but through commitment to all life. I walked down the golden stairs and into the elevator. There were two large buttons, with small buttons in between. The one large button resembled the sun and the other a photograph of the earth from outer space. I selected earth and returned, still perceiving the brightness of the One shining as this transparent rainbow universe. Once again I became faintly aware of Mother Serena reading the names of those to whom she was sending healing light and love. Perhaps because of her presence, so deeply involved in the activity of compassion, I had been able to understand the profound role compassionate love plays in the spiritual process. I could now understand how the traditional mystical vision of the insubstantiality of the universe and its beings, this mere rainbow inside a bubble, can coexist with love for beings and commitment to the universe. I could also understand how, for Plotinus, the realms of Being proceed inevitably from the superabundance of the One, because the floating bubble, with its rainbow structure of Being, was generated simply from the supersaturation of pure awareness by itself. And I could understand what Plotinus means when he remarks: *The One is born, so to speak, to Its own interior as if in love of the clear light which is Itself, and It is what It loves.* For no individual *I* had been returned into the bubble of Being. This apparent journey inward and downward was simply the eternal overflow or emanation of the One as Being or Love.

CHAPTER SIX

THE LANDSCAPE
THAT LAUGHS

*Jewish Soul Masters of
the Hasidic Way*

As one enters the realm of holy ecstasy, the philosophical enterprise catches fire. When questioned about rational proof for God's existence, a soul master picked up the sacred Torah and exclaimed, *I swear that God exists. Do you need anything else?* From someone who consciously lives and moves in God, this is a truly convincing demonstration of Divine Presence, for it *is* Divine Presence. Once thought and perception are ignited by the ecstatic flame of a *soul on fire*, as Elie Wiesel describes the Hasidic masters, we become conscious of God's Life living through us and can no more doubt God's existence than we can doubt our own.

This mystery of Divine Life lived secretly through human life is revealed in the Jewish mystical tradition of Kabbalah. Kabbalistic wisdom is ordinarily shared only among elite circles, but the Hasidic masters are illumined beings who, in the abandon of ecstasy, share with all thirsty souls the secret that human life can disappear into Divine Presence while still being lived on the earthly plane. While the traditional Kabbalist moves toward this secret union with the Divine through esoteric study and contemplation in solitude, the Hasidic master disappears into God's Life by transforming ordinary daily existence into the holy dance of ecstasy, by perceiving God only.

This approach of *God only*, because of its intense simplicity, can be difficult to appreciate. We may fear that the fire of ecstasy will consume our ability to think rationally. Yet the ecstasy of Divine Life is a warm, sweet flame that irradiates our thinking process, rather than turning it to ashes. And the soul master can communicate this ecstasy directly, as one candle is lit from another. Wiesel reports the words of a Hasidic disciple concerning his *rebbe*, or spiritual guide: *No matter how hardened, how icy your soul may be, at his touch it will burst into flames.*

Israel Baal Shem Tov was a holy teacher, living in Eastern Europe from about 1700 to 1760, who reawakened the Hasidic flame in Jewish tradition, the flame of ecstasy which often remains hidden in the glowing coals of orthodox practice of Torah. The details of his life survive only in legendary tales, but he appears to have been one of several Baal Shems, or Masters of the Name, who were wandering saints, healers, and visionaries. The Baal Shem Tov, judging from the powerful lineage of soul masters he generated, was never destined to be an obscure sage or shaman. Although Jewish tradition has crystallized in such a way that new prophets are not allowed to appear, the Baal Shem Tov may be regarded as a holy figure comparable in stature to the biblical prophet Elijah. Any crystallized religious tradition can be melted by the fire of ecstasy, allowing Divine Presence to flow again in all its original power. This release of holy power, this rediscovery of the fullness of Divine Life abiding in the human heart, occurred with dramatic intensity through the Baal Shem Tov, his disciples, and the lineage of soul masters that flows from him.

Elie Wiesel tells a story about the Baal Shem and his mystical intimacy with the prophet Elijah. *One day the Baal Shem promised his disciples to show them the prophet Elijah. "Open your eyes wide," he said. A few days later they saw a beggar enter the*

House of Study and emerge clutching a book under his arm. Shortly thereafter they watched him leaving a ceremony, taking along a silver spoon. The third time he appeared to them disguised as a soldier on a horse, asking them to light his pipe. "It was he," said the Baal Shem. *"The secret is in the eyes."* Through this living parable of the beggar soldier, the Baal Shem was not suggesting that everyone is Elijah, but that everyone can be. If God wills to manifest Elijah—holy ecstasy or Divine Presence—through any particular being, it can be done. This is the revolutionary stance of the Hasidic Way.

The Hasidic Way, like the Tantric Way, is ecstatic celebration of the Divine Life which lives through all lives. This celebration rises beyond the limits imposed by conventional religiousness, and yet remains rooted in intense commitment to the practice of *mitzvah,* to the ways of holy living revealed through the Torah. This spiritual discipline prepares the practitioner to embrace life with holy ecstasy rather than viscerally or selfishly. Wiesel tells the story of how a certain rebbe became the disciple of the Maggid of Mezeritch, who was one of the Baal Shem's direct disciples. This rebbe, like the Maggid before him, embraced the Hasidic Way of Divine Celebration only after rigorous discipline. *For years he had lived in seclusion, refusing to meet people so as not to take time away from Torah. One day he heard a Hasid quote the Maggid's interpretation of Umala haaretz kinvanekha, the earth is full of things that permit man to acquire partnership with God. . . . He climbed out the nearest window and hurried to Mezeritch. Later he told the famous Goan of Vilna: "What I learned in Mezeritch? One simple truth: vehai bahem, Torah is given to man so he may celebrate life."*

A mathematical formula, a headache, the death of a loved one, a child's game, a religious ceremony—each permits us *to acquire partnership with God* when experienced ecstatically, when celebrated as God's own Life. If the universe were fundamentally separate from the Divine, true partnership or union with God would be impossible. But since the universe *is* God's Life, our own life, our own mind, our own dream is an open door to the Divine. All life is only Divine Life, and each moment or situation can be used to awaken partnership or union with God. Writes Wiesel: *The Maggid interpreted the Talmudic saying Veda ma lemala mimkha as follows: veda, know that, ma lemala, what occurs up above, mimkha, derives from you as well. Whatever the event, you are its origin; it is through you, through your will, that God manifests Himself.* God is dreaming the universe through the souls of all beings, themselves sparks of the Divine, like an endless Hasidic story, rich in spiritual meaning, mysterious in design.

If our life is to be celebrated as God's Life, how are we to understand the suffering that permeates human existence? This is the instinctive question that arises in all theistic traditions: why is there suffering if God is all-powerful and all-good? Wiesel reports the following form of this question and its solution, or dissolution, by an illumined soul master in the lineage of the Baal Shem Tov. This rebbe, Zusia, was heavily burdened by illness and other problems. He was asked how he could continue to praise God. In the mood of ecstatic love, he responded: *Who is suffering? Not I. I am happy. Zusia is happy to live in the world that God, blessed be He, created. Zusia lacks nothing, needs nothing . . . and his heart is filled with gratitude.* When holy ecstasy is deep enough, the question *Who is suffering?* has no answer, for the individual is immersed in Divine Presence, and therefore the question *Why suffering?* dissolves. But this revelation occurs only on the level of ecstasy, not on the level of pious or rational explanation. Zusia recognized that he was sick and burdened with all kinds of suffering. He did not close his eyes to the facts of daily experience. But he perceived Divine Presence throughout these painful situations. He mystically understood existence in all its infinite detail as welling up with divine Plentitude, not as alienated from the Divine. On another occasion Zusia responded in a different mood to the question of suffering: *True, suffering exists, but like everything else, it, too, comes from God. . . . Man is too weak to accept or absorb divine love, which is absolute. For that reason, and that reason alone, does God cover it with the veil that is pain.* This

response, too, can be assimilated only in the mood of openness to revelation, not as an explanation. The mystery of
Divine Life is to be lived, not explained.

Zusia speaks of our suffering or pain as a Divine veil but
suffering also removes the human veils by which we have
obscured the Divine Life living through us. The soul master
does not seek to avoid or to escape suffering but purposefully
accepts suffering to unveil the intrinsic freedom of the soul.
Wiesel gives this illustration of the voluntary suffering of
Zusia: *He came to an inn and noticed birds in a cage. Naturally
he freed them. Birds are meant to fly. And naturally the innkeeper
thought otherwise and gave him a lesson without words. No matter,
here was Zusia, back on the road, his body aching but his spirits
high, carefree and deliriously happy.* The soul master, with every
act, creates a parable. This is a story of liberation from the
cage of mundane thinking that confines our consciousness
and prevents the ecstatic flight that is natural to it. The innkeeper represents not only oppressive social institutions and
personality structures but also the universe itself when regarded as a place of suffering, sickness, and death. What
releases us from our imprisonment is the ecstasy of Divine
Life, focused through such an illumined being as Zusia, who
in the face of suffering remains fearless and free.

Suffering clears access to the ecstatic experience of the
soul's intrinsic freedom. As a spiritual discipline attuning one
to the Divine, suffering is to be cultivated rather than to be
escaped. Padre Pio, who for some thirty years during the
present century manifested continuously the five wounds,
or stigmata, of Christ, made this simple but radical statement:
*If you but knew the value of your sufferings, you would pray fer-
vently that they not be removed from you.* Such a prayer must
reflect the authentic longing to be purified or freed, not the
neurotic pattern of clinging to our suffering. Suffering should
be embraced under the spiritual guidance of someone who
lives in holy ecstasy, who knows how to use all we encounter
as a path to the Divine.

Guidance from the illumined soul master, the rebbe or *tzaddik*, is considered essential in the Hasidic Way. While repeating *all life is God's Life*, we could drown in our own selfish tendencies. The spiritual guide must show us how to swim through the powerful waves of Divine Life, stripping away our secret fears and obsessions, allowing us to discover our own natural buoyancy or ecstasy. The tzaddik lives every moment in the ecstatic perception of *God only*. Every act of the tzaddik, such as Zusia's freeing of the birds, shows his disciples how to live and move in God's Life, providing a teaching deeper than words can convey. Writes Wiesel: *Leib, son of Sarah . . . proclaimed to anyone willing to listen: "I came to the Maggid not to listen to discourses. . . . I came to watch him tie his shoelaces."* These illumined beings are the living Torah, God's invitation to humanity to awaken into Divine Life. Wiesel describes the tzaddik: *He is what man can be, wants to be. He is the chosen one who is refused nothing, in heaven or on earth. God is angry? He can make God smile.* This intimacy of the tzaddik with the Divine amounts to a sharing of God's own nature. And this Divine Life lived on earth by the illumined human being is not an isolated miracle but represents, as Wiesel suggests, *what man can be.*

Each disciple of the tzaddik aspires to live God's Life, but the process of discipleship is long and arduous, involving total trust in the illumined teacher. Continues Wiesel: *His followers owe him blind and unconditional allegiance. . . . To question the Rebbe is worse than sin; it is absurd, for it destroys the very relationship that binds you to him.* This veneration of the spiritual teacher releases one from the sense of personal control. In the path of ecstasy, one does not take the ultimate responsibility to establish what is coherent and what is not, but plunges into Divine Presence. It is *absurd*, in Wiesel's terms, for the disciple to question the authentic tzaddik, or Enlightened soul master, as it is superfluous for the ecstatic to question Divine Presence, simply because there can exist no duality of questioner and questioned when God's Life alone is being lived. The master becomes for the disciple an actual revelation of Divine Presence.

One cannot rationally evaluate the Divine, which is pure mystery. As Wiesel continues: *If the Rebbe's behavior appears bizarre, it means that the Hasid does not possess the required powers of understanding. . . . A superior, almost a perfect being . . . he uses his mysterious powers to redeem the sins of his generation.* The Enlightened being, or tzaddik, is a redeemer, a full reflection on the earthly plane of the Divine. Yet the tzaddik possesses a complete human nature, which, though released or transcended, is warmly and expressively present. The presence in the illumined being of a full human nature is the vehicle for God's redeeming power, which must be focused fully through our earthly life in order to transfigure it. Wiesel remarks about the tzaddik: *His suffering confers a meaning upon all suffering; and when he eats, he cleanses the very act of nourishing the body.* Human nature is thus cleansed or freed to be a perfect natural channel for the expression of God's Life.

The Hasidic soul master uses clairvoyance and other powers which we encounter in the lives of shamans and saints from all cultures. Wiesel tells of the clairvoyant guidance offered by the Baal Shem to a boy of eleven: *The Baal Shem looked at the boy searchingly and began to tell him a story that some of those present forgot immediately and whose hidden meaning eluded the others; only he, little Menahem-Mendl, remembered the tale in all its details and understood its significance: it was his life's story, from its first to its last day. . . . Later, whenever his health worried his friends, he would reassure them: "I still have one half, or one quarter of the way to go."* The Baal Shem perceived in accurate detail the entire spiritual unfoldment of this boy. This is why obedience to the guru, or tzaddik, of this stature is not an abdication of responsibility but an opening into a deeper sense of coherence.

I once heard a first-hand account of this guiding and redeeming power which is focused through illumined human beings in every culture. Swami Satprakashananda told me of being a young boy when the famous monk Vivekananda visited East Bengal in 1901. At the arrival ceremony, there were thousands crowded around Vivekananda, who was so garlanded that the boy could glimpse only the top of his head from a distance. But this twelve-year-old child's longing to meet the great saint face to face was fulfilled in a remarkable way some days later, when he went to the riverbank to see the country boat in which Vivekananda had taken a short cruise. Much to the boy's amazement, he saw the famous disciple of Ramakrishna pacing back and forth in the cabin of the boat, which was surrounded by windows. There was no one with him. The child sat on the sloping mud bank of the river, at eye level with the cabin, and watched Vivekananda moving like a lion, a three-day growth of beard enhancing the intensity of his expression. Suddenly the saint stopped and walked to the open window nearest the boy. Emphatically and purposefully, Vivekananda placed his elbow on the window sill and his chin on his palm. He stared at the boy for perhaps two minutes and then returned to pacing. The boy never met Vivekananda again but eventually became a monk in the order founded by Vivekananda, and an illumined scholar of the Advaita Vedanta philosophy, which was Vivekananda's own special focus. This is the power of the tzaddik: one gaze confirmed and energized the entire spiritual unfoldment of that boy of twelve. In the presence of such a person, our presuppositions are dissolved. There is no need for an effort at surrender, nor are there pressing doubts about the teacher's authenticity. This is the transmission from the Divine through the tzaddik.

The ultimate manifestation of the Divine through the human is the Messiah. The followers of the Hasidic Way are always expecting the appearance of the Messiah. This poignant expectancy is an intense spiritual practice that purifies the entire daily consciousness, transforming conventional or mundane thinking into an ecstatic waiting in Divine Presence. Since the coming of the Messiah is regarded as imminent, this practice generates a spiritual mood that resembles the inwardness and expectancy of a pregnant woman. Carrying the image further, we are all pregnant with the Messiah. As our spiritual life ripens, we can feel the Messiah Nature moving within us. The tzaddik has actually given mystical birth to this inner Messiah, whose Presence now radiates through the illumined master in a way that is intuitively perceptible by the sensitive Hasid or disciple.

To the tzaddik, the Messiah nature manifests fully, though secretly, in the present while still offering the promise of universal manifestation in the future. Having committed oneself to the purifying practice of waiting for the Messiah as a future manifestation, one is gradually transformed by the realization that the Messiah has secretly come, not simply through each authentic soul master but also through every person who is faithfully waiting. This realization of the Messiah nature mystically present at the core of our human nature is what actually constitutes the tzaddik. Knowing that Divine Presence is perfectly, though secretly, expressed through humanity, the soul master can heal and sanctify simply by envisioning our intrinsic wholeness and sanctity.

The manifestation of the Messiah nature through the tzaddik is subtle, recognized only by ecstatic lovers of God. Disguised from the world, appearing even as a tramp or a madcap, the tzaddik carries on the mystical function of the Messiah, the regathering or reawakening into conscious Godhead of the sparks of Divine Nature that are scattered as creation and remain unconscious or dreaming. Wiesel describes Rebbe Nachman's disguise and his mystical function: *His fierce individualism irked many. So did his pronounced taste for mystery and ambiguity, his disdain of public opinion. . . . To pull a man out of the mud, the Just Man must set foot into that mud. . . . To lead back lost souls, he must leave the comfort of his home and seek them wherever they might be. "In every man, there is something of the Messiah." In every man, in every place. The Kabbalah says it, the mystics repeat it. To free mankind one must gather the sparks, all the sparks, and integrate them into the sacred flame.*

Simultaneously with the mystical appreciation of the Messiah Nature transmitted through the tzaddik, there continues to exist the expectation of the powerful, kingly Messiah. When he appears, the entire planet will be transformed in a flash of illumination, not just inwardly, as is already occurring, but outwardly and openly. No matter how many centuries pass according to human reckoning, this universal revelation remains always an imminent future. The Hasid lives with this future Event so intimately that it pervades the present. Wiesel describes Rebbe Menahem-Mendl: *Like all Hasidic Masters, he lived wholly in his expectation of the Messiah's coming. Mornings he would go to the widow, look outside and sadly remark: "He has not yet come, for the world is still the same."* The secret inner Messiah Nature which awakens in the illumined tzaddik sleeps within all living beings or sparks of the Divine. When Menahem-Mendl remarks of the Messiah, *He has not yet come, for the world is still the same,* this does not mean that the tzaddik fails to experience the inward presence of the Messiah Nature. It simply means that the awakened rebbe realistically perceives human beings still living in their conventional, unillumined consciousness, although the Messiah Nature is secretly irradiating all beings, ready to manifest to individuals the moment they open in holy ecstasy.

There are two aspects of the Enlightened soul master, as there are for all human beings: Messiah Nature and human nature. For those who have not yet experienced deep spiritual awakening, the Messiah Nature is to one degree or another obscured by the human nature. When the illumined person becomes aware of Divine Presence as the core of human nature, he or she does not transcend the human context, which involves unavoidable limits of perspective, both cultural and personal. Regardless of these limits, however, the Enlightened, or God-realized, person is genuinely one with the Divine, as a particular tongue of flame is not separate from the fire.

We find a reticence in Jewish tradition to express openly this oneness with God which we can call God-realization. But hints are given. Wiesel reports that when questioned about the nature of the tzaddik, or God-realized being, *Rebbe Nachman would answer that a Tzaddik is comparable to the Creator and not to His creature.* Yet human limits are not erased by God-realization, or Enlightenment. Rebbe Nachman himself discredits the popular religious notion that the tzaddik is limitless or omniscient: *There are two erroneous concepts going around the world. The first: that a Just Man cannot make a mistake; and the second: that he cannot remain great even if he has made a mistake.* God-realized, or Enlightened, beings can make mistakes. The notion of a human individual not subject to some limitations of understanding and cultural preference is a religious fantasy. Though irradiated with wisdom and power beyond our ordinary imagination, God-realized beings are working still through the human structure, where certain physical, cultural, and temperamental limits are natural. There is no wood without some grain. Yet the fact of their limitation does not mean that we can judge or evaluate these Enlightened beings from our more limited sphere of understanding. While our limitations remain a source of confusion and suffering to ourselves and to others, the human limitations of God-realized beings become channels of blessing to the particular culture and historical period in which they appear.

Wiesel tells a beautiful Hasidic story that illustrates the difference between our ordinary human nature and the Divine Nature at its core. Eizik is a pious Jew who suffers severe poverty. He sincerely prays to God for help but receives no apparent response. Then he begins to experience the recurring dream that there is a glorious treasure awaiting him in the great city, distant from his small town. At first he considers the dream nonsense and concludes that he must be delirious. But the dream continues to repeat itself vividly:

the treasure is hidden under a particular bridge. Eizik, son of Yekel, finally decides to travel to the city in order to free himself from this strange obsession. After much hardship, he arrives and discovers a perfect correspondence with his dream. While standing in amazement beneath the very bridge where the treasure was to have been unearthed, he is arrested by soldiers guarding the bridge. Out of desperation, Eizik relates his dream to the captain of the guard, who, amused by the peasant's credulity, releases him with the admonition never again to believe in dreams. As an example, the captain cites his own absurd experience: a recurrent dream that treasure was to be found beneath the stove of a certain Eizik, son of Yekel, in a small town distant from the city. Bemused, Eizik travels home and finds the gold beneath his own stove.

The treasure is at home. The Messiah Nature is hidden beneath our human nature. Yet the revelatory process is never simple or direct, but resembles this story of Eizik. Awakening to our own Divine Nature is not achieved automatically by going through certain steps in a sacred system, by prayers or meditations or rituals, no matter how sincere we may be. Ecstasy must first burn away these efforts at grasping God, leaving us only with apparent nonsense: the dream of Divine treasure somewhere distant from our ordinary consciousness. Then there occurs the arduous journey and the incredible sharing of dreams with the tzaddik, or soul master. Whatever bizarre or sublime form the holy presence may choose to assume and to speak through, It redirects us to our original home, to the priceless Divine spark of our intrinsic nature.

There is intense humor to this circular quest for Divine treasure, not in the midst of its seriousness or even anguish, but from the illumined perspective of the one who has finally returned home. Elie Wiesel writes about the stories of Rebbe Nachman: *Laughter occupies an astonishingly important place in his work. Here and there, one meets a man who laughs and does nothing else. Also a landscape that laughs. We* encounter this same holy laughter in an account of kensho, or Enlightenment, recorded by a contemporary Japanese practitioner: *At midnight I abruptly awakened. At first my mind was foggy, then suddenly that quotation flashed into my consciousness: "I came to realize clearly that Mind is no other than mountains, rivers, and the great wide earth, the sun and the moon and the stars."* As in the case of Eizik, son of Yekel, the jewel of Original Mind, the treasure of Divine Nature, is discovered at home in the realm of primal awareness, which appears as rivers, mountains, stars, and persons. The transcendent humor of this discovery is overwhelming. Continues the Zen practitioner: *Instantaneously, like surging waves, a tremendous delight welled up in me, a veritable hurricane of delight, as I laughed loudly and wildly: Ha, ha, ha, ha, ha, ha! There's no reasoning here, no reasoning at all! Ha, ha, ha! The empty sky split into two, then opened its enormous mouth and began to laugh uproariously: Ha, ha, ha!* Rebbe Nachman, the European Jew of the late-eighteenth century, and this contemporary Japanese Buddhist both encounter a landscape that laughs. There is no fundamental cultural separation: ecstasy is ecstasy, fire is fire.

This ecstatic laughter of Enlightenment is perfectly expressed by Rebbe Nachman's own words: *Once upon a time there was a country that encompassed all the countries of the world. And in that country, there was a town that incorporated all the towns of the country; and in that town there was a street in which were gathered all the streets of the town; and on that street there was a house that sheltered all the houses of the street; and in that house there was a room, and in that room there was a man, and that man personified all men of all countries, and that man laughed and laughed—no one had ever laughed like that before.* This is the clear laughter of Enlightenment that perceives all countries, towns, streets, and beings as Original Mind or as God's Dream. That is how Rebbe Nachman greeted and even welcomed the pirates, prisons, and plagues he encountered during a chaotic pilgrimage he once made to the Holy Land: all his patterns of rational expectation had crumbled away in the ecstasy of *God only*. He lived wholly in the Divine landscape that laughs. *There is no reasoning here: Ha, Ha, ha!* Zusia opens the cage and the birds fly away free.

In the midst of this transcendental laughter, however, the illumined soul master maintains deep contact with human beings and their earthly dilemma. We encounter in Jewish spirituality a parallel to the Bodhisattva of Mahayana Buddhism, an Enlightened being fully committed to returning again and again into planetary life, reincarnating not from selfish desire but from compassion for living beings, concern for their Enlightenment. In the Jewish context, this is expressed as an eternal solidarity with the Chosen People in their pilgrimage through history to the Holy Land or illumination. This focus of love and commitment upon the earth rather than in the transcendental Divine is mystically expressed by Rebbe Nachman through one of his tales: *In the center of the world there is a mountain and on this mountain there is a rock and out of this rock there spouts a spring. Well, everything has a heart. Even the world has a heart, a heart that is a complete being with face, hands, legs, eyes, and ears. And this heart is full of fire and anxious to go back to the spring, at the other end of the world, at the other side of the abyss. This heart is doubly unfortunate; the sun pursues it and dries it. To survive, it contemplates the spring. But the longer it contemplates the spring, the greater its desire. Yet, as soon as it comes closer to the mountain, the peak disappears, and with it, the spring. And then its soul leaves, for it lives only in the love it feels for the spring. And if it were to stop, the whole world would be reduced to nothingness. Thus it must remain far away, on the other side, protected by a bird, its wings spread wide.*

Interpreting freely, this Mountain may be understood as the absolutely transcendent Godhead, void even of existence. From this Absolute One, focused through the Rock which is Being, overflows the Spring, which is the personal God, the God of Love. The human soul is described here by Rebbe Nachman as the *heart of the world*. The parable speaks of this

Heart, or humanity, as full of fire and anxious to return to the Spring. This is the fire of ecstatic longing which fuels the human quest to merge with the Divine Beloved in that mystical union which alone can quench our thirst for wholeness. The attraction between the child and the parents and the attraction between sexual partners are outer reflections of this inner longing for wholeness, providing us clues to the holy quest from our ordinary human experience. The essence of the entire structure of human longing is the secret desire to swim in the Spring of Divine Love. But this Spring, as the parable reveals, lies on the other side of the Abyss of relative existence. The Sun represents the suffering, inherent in existence, which pursues and dries up the Heart. But this blast of sunlight also serves our spiritual evolution by intensifying our longing to merge into the coolness of the Spring. To survive, continues the parable, the Heart contemplates the Spring of Divine Love. But as contemplation gradually intensifies and the contemplative draws closer and closer to the Mountain, the Peak and the Spring disappear: radical transcendence swallows up the Divine Beloved and the human soul *leaves*, or merges into the void of Godhead. The soul's individuality is simply the longing it feels for the Spring of God's Love. Were this longing to be fulfilled, there would be no more world, because the human world, even the entire universe, is a creation out of this basic longing. The whole of our existence is a rich Hasidic tale, with infinite meanings, dreamed by the Divine through the longing Heart which is humanity.

Contemplation of this Tale of Existence is not to be consummated by disappearance into Nirvana, Godhead, or Void. The Bodhisattva and the Hasid desire to be born again and again among the People, among the human family, not from nostalgia but from solidarity with all life. Thus, Rebbe Nachman's parable continues, the soul cannot allow itself to be lost in Godhead by approaching too near the Spring of Divine Love. But the soul remains protected from the intense suffering of relative existence under cooling shade of two Great

Wings: the Torah, or teaching of Divine Presence, and the tzaddik, or awakened one, in whom this teaching is fully brought to life. But such spiritual protection is not magical exemption from suffering. Reading Rebbe Nachman's account of his own chaotic pilgrimage to the Holy Land, we can perceive how the Hasid or the Bodhisattva takes upon himself or herself all the suffering of the world, transforming it into the ecstasy of *God only*.

Vowing to reincarnate is extremely difficult when one has clearly understood the flaws of human existence and has directly experienced the spiritual beauty of the Divine Realm. This hard decision to remain on earth, to focus one's spiritual life on the earthly plane, is poignantly expressed by Rebbe Leib, who recounts the reluctance of his soul to accept physical embodiment. His words are not simply metaphorical but reflect actual mystical experience of the transcendent Divine Realm: *Before I was born, I refused life. What is the good of toiling among mortals, who are prey to their own weaknesses? . . . Do you know who finally made me change my mind? A peasant with a shovel in his hands who accosted me as though I were an old acquaintance. "Hey, you," he said, "take a good look: I work without respite to give a little joy, a little rest to people who sorely need it. And what do you do? You lie around here as if creation had no human purpose. Why do you refuse to help me?" You see, added the Rebbe, I could resist the angels but not him. Because, well . . . Do you know who he was? Yes, it was the Baal Shem himself.* The Baal Shem is a rare world teacher, who not only appeared on the earth but still wanders through higher planes of Being, convincing illumined souls to come down to this world rather than simply remaining lost to heavenly contemplation. *Take birth to kindle holy ecstasy among all sentient beings*, calls the Baal Shem.

Ramakrishna experienced a vision of the similar process by which his Enlightened disciple, Vivekananda, had been enticed to take birth for the spiritual welfare of humanity. In this vision, Vivekananda appeared as an archetypal sage, rapt in contemplation within a transcendental realm close to the Mountain of the Absolute. The golden light of this realm appeared to condense into the form of a small child, who began sweetly and playfully drawing Vivekananda back to the awareness of relativity. Simply because the child was so delightful, the transcendent sage could not resist. The child—who was none other than Ramakrishna, as the peasant with the shovel was none other than the Baal Shem—remarked simply and lovingly, *I am going down. Come help me.* The sage reluctantly agreed.

This solidarity with living beings need not be expressed metaphysically or mystically. In fact, it thrives best in the most earthly surroundings. Wiesel tells a story about Rebbe Wolfe: *He was attending a circumcision. Stepping outside for a moment, he noticed the coachman shivering with cold. . . . "Go in, warm yourself, have a drink and something to eat."—"Who will watch the horses?"—"I will." The coachman did as the Master wished. Several hours later people saw Rebbe Wolfe, half frozen in the snow, jumping from one foot to the other, at a loss to understand why the guests were making such a fuss.* Unhesitating, unpremeditated solidarity with fellow beings is perhaps the most vivid expression of Enlightenment. This loving compassion is ecstatic, free from rational calculation concerning how much help one might realistically be able to give. But, as holy ecstasy, it gives the gift of itself, which is, in Hasidic terms, God's Life. There is no help more far-reaching, practical, or profound.

The ecstasy of the Hasidic Way, which often appears as nonsense or madness to mundane understanding, pervaded the lives of biblical prophets such as Jeremiah as well as the Baal Shem and the soul masters whom his lineage has produced. Wiesel evokes the prophetic flavor of Levi-Yitzhak: *Once, he climbed to the roof of a building facing the marketplace. He watched the merchants buying and selling and suddenly he began to shout at the top of his lungs: "Good people, do not forget, do not forget that God, too, is to be feared!"* This soul master was genuinely lost in the holy ecstasy through which his will became transparent to God's Will, his words became God's Words. Through the prophetic being, the Divine speaks in human language for all to hear. Wiesel continues to describe this ecstatic rebbe: *Accompanying his dead son to the cemetery he began to dance, crying: "Lord, you entrusted me my son with a pure soul and that is how I give him back to You."* Holy ecstasy dances spontaneously. The ecstatic one is not concealing some inner pain or despair with his or her dance. The dance is not conceived as a talisman to be used against suffering and death. Suffering and death have disappeared completely into Divine Presence. God projects the soul, which is a perfectly pure expression of the Divine Nature, and then withdraws the soul into its Source: this outbreath and inbreath are God's ecstatic dance as Life. Levi-Yitzhak simply radiated that Divine Dance. *He worshiped with such abandon that the frightened faithful instinctively moved away. He gesticulated, howled, and danced, jumping from one corner to the other, pushing and overturning whatever was in his way. People ceased to exist for him. When he prayed, he himself ceased to exist.*

This is the Divine revealing itself through the human: the individual disappears into holy ecstasy, re-emerges, and then disappears again as the inbreath and outbreath of Divine Plenitude itself. Such intense intimacy with the Divine can deepen into complete mystical union. Consider what Rebbe Nachman says about the I-Thou relationship, the devotional metaphor by which the experience of God's Presence is most often expressed in Jewish tradition: *If I am and You are because I am myself and You are Yourself, then I am I and You are You.* This is the conventional understanding of the I-Thou relationship, on the human level as well as between the human and the Divine. Rebbe Nachman continues: *But if I am because You are, I am not I and You are not You.* This is the ecstatic I-Thou, the love play of Divine Plenitude with Itself as God and Hasid. In this ecstasy, the I stands outside the I and the Thou outside the Thou. The I and the Thou, no longer fundamentally separate, become intimate friends: they quarrel, play hide-and-seek, merge in union, and re-emerge in conversation—all the while knowing that *I am not I and You are not You,* for the apparent barrier between human and Divine has dissolved.

Elie Wiesel writes of Rebbe Nachman: *"The angels never repeat their litanies,"* he said, quoting the Talmud. *And he went on to explain: "The angels praising the Lord are never the same; the Lord changes them every day." Rebbe Nachman's conclusion: "Whoever repeats himself displeases God and moves away from Him."* We indulge in a basic repetition of ourselves when we insist *I, I, I—I am this separate individual.* The only way not to repeat ourselves is to be the ecstasy that continually overflows all barriers between human beings as well as between the Divine and the human. When we are immersed in Divine Presence, our individuality remains, but it is released from its repetitive or confining nature. We become flames in the dancing fire of holy ecstasy.

CHAPTER SEVEN

THE NEW AEON HAS DAWNED

Letters of Saint Paul

Paul was an ecstatic rabbi for whom the Messiah had actually come. Like many Jewish masters of the Hasidic Way, Paul began his spiritual life with intense commitment to orthodox practice of the Holy Law. He sternly opposed the charismatic Jewish sect that believed the Messiah promised by prophetic tradition had appeared as Christ Jesus. From Paul's perspective, Jesus had been simply one of several wandering teachers and madcaps of the day, such as John the Baptist. Paul traveled the countryside persecuting these Christians, condemning to imprisonment men and women of this heterodox Jewish sect who promised that the Kingdom of God would soon descend upon earth. Then, suddenly, this brilliant scholar and dedicated practitioner of orthodoxy joined the Christian Jews, turning all his eloquence and zeal toward justifying and propagating a Messianic movement of simple rural people.

Ecstatic awakening to the Messiah, or Christ Nature, was experienced by Christian Jews through the fully illumined being, Jesus of Nazareth. After the death of Jesus, this process intensified. The master's radiant form appeared to devoted followers in dreams and waking visions. His invisible spiritual presence was felt unmistakably whenever Christian Jews gathered to pray. This Divine Power, or Presence, was subliminally communicated to Paul through his prolonged exposure to Christian ecstasy in the role of persecutor. On the road to Damascus, Paul's resistance finally dissolved and the boundless radiance of the Messiah, or Christ Nature, opened before his inner vision suddenly and with such intensity that physical sight became impossible for three days. Divine Radiance emanates a subtle resonance which saints of various cultures hear speaking to them in their own languages. This inner voice revealed to Paul that Jesus of Nazareth had indeed been a full expression of the Christ Nature, the Divine Radiance which abides secretly at the core of human nature.

Through this experience of Enlightenment, Paul was empowered to transmit Christ as Divine Power and Presence, not to preach Jesus as a human being. We do not encounter in Paul's letters any references to the parables and miracles of Jesus, who is not envisioned simply as a historical individual. Paul's only focus on the life of Jesus is the Crucifixion and the Resurrection: the attenuation of human nature and the consequent dawning of Divine Nature through the human body and mind. The events of Crucifixion and Resurrection are envisioned as occurring inwardly for all those who mystically *die* to human limits and *rise* as Divine Radiance. Paul thus initiated an apostolic succession which is mystical, which does not depend on the physical touch of Jesus, whom he never met nor on detailed knowledge of Jesus as a historical individual. Paul's spiritual transmission leads outside history into the Divine Radiance at the core of our conscious being. We are as close to this Christ Nature now as Paul was during his lifetime. Intervening centuries produce only the psychological illusion of distance. The Kingdom of God is among us. What Paul terms the *Old Aeon* is dissolving. The *New Aeon* has already dawned.

Paul was given the prophetic role of revealing the Messiah, or Christ, who lives secretly in all hearts, not only to his own beloved People but to all nations. The open secret of Paul's teaching is the mystical union with Christ, which was revealed to him on the road to Damascus. Mystical union is usually an esoteric teaching made known only to a small circle of initiates. With generosity and abandon, Paul openly proclaimed what he called *life in Christ* to all segments of the Jewish community and even to the gentile world. Paul never suggested that certain individuals or cultures were not spiritually evolved enough to share the mystery of union with Christ, although he did refer to *infants in Christ,* implying that there are various levels of experiencing and understanding this union.

Exclaims Paul in a letter to his disciples at Colossae: *I want you to know that I do have to struggle hard for you . . . to stir your minds, so that your understanding may come to full development, until you really know God's secret, God's mystery of Christ.* We will not be able to appreciate the nature of this secret teaching, however, unless we understand Christ to be the Divine Radiance at the core of our being, rather than simply the historical person Jesus of Nazareth. For Paul, the secret that our intrinsic nature is the Christ Nature need not take years of intense purification and meditation to experience and to understand. This inner Christ has been made accessible to all by the flood of Divine Grace focused through Jesus which Paul understood as the dawning of a New Aeon, or New Age. This transfiguration of human civilization and even of the physical universe renders all beings transparent to the Divine Radiance at their core. In this New Aeon, the deep secret of our Divine Nature rises to the surface of consciousness. Yet, because this gift of Christ Nature is offered equally to all, regardless of special effort or qualification, it is difficult to accept for those who consider themselves advanced in religious observance or philosophical training. This is why Paul speaks of life in Christ as *an obstacle to the Jews and madness to the Greeks.*

Regardless of its complete simplicity and accessibility to all, the union with Christ that Paul teaches is Gnosis, the highest liberating wisdom. Thus Paul speaks about *God's mystery of Christ, in which all the jewels of Wisdom and Knowledge are hidden.* The path of wisdom is well described by the words attributed to Jesus: *Know the Truth and the Truth will set you free.* We do not achieve freedom from our human limits by performing righteous deeds or ritual acts but by knowing the truth about our own ultimate nature as Divine Nature. Paul's Gnosis is radical: no human effort can attain freedom, not even the effort to know. Following the paradigm of his own experience on the road to Damascus, Paul teaches that liberation from our limited human nature can occur only through Divine Grace.

For Paul, the Messiah's Coming fundamentally dissolved Jewish Law and, by extension, all other culturally based moral and religious codes. Many Hasidic teachers verge on proclaiming this same radical truth: when the Messiah appears, the Law will be spontaneously fulfilled and thereby dissolved. Paul was consistently Jewish in his thinking. The only factor that renders him unorthodox is his conviction, grounded in ecstatic experience, that the Messiah has actually come and is coming again. The Coming of the Messiah is an event that orthodox Jewish tradition never allows to occur, no matter how many Messiah figures may appear, just as, by orthodox Christianity, no Second Coming of Christ could be widely accepted, for its authenticity would be denied, as Jesus was rejected by the religious leaders of his day. To the assertion that the Messiah has come, an orthodox Jew would respond: *It is still the same world of suffering. How could the Messiah have come?* This reflects the conventional idea of the Messiah's transformation of the Old into the New Aeon. By contrast, esoteric wisdom, or Gnosis, understands the Messiah's Coming as an inner, secret, mystical transfiguration of Being. We are still living on the same imperfect earthly plane, but at the core of our being an entirely new order or orientation has been revealed.

The experience of this dawning of the New Aeon is spoken of by Paul as our mystical union with Christ. In the intensity of this spiritual experience, Paul exclaims, *I live now not with my own life but with the life of Christ who lives in me.* This ecstatic union reveals Divine Power and Presence as the source or ground of our consciousness. During ecstasy, Holy Presence irradiates us so completely that we disappear as independent persons, although the afterimage of body and mind remains. Paul's imagery often evokes the Divine as ground or foundation. He exhorts his disciples at Colossae: *Be rooted in Christ. Be built on Him.* Paul is here suggesting the same mystical oneness reflected in the words of Jesus: *I am the Vine and you are the branches.* There is no distinction in intrinsic nature between the vine and its branches. Paul continues: *In Christ lives the fullness of Divinity, and in Him you find your own fulfillment.* Our mystical completion or fulfillment is realization that the Godhead lives fully through us. Paul does not advise seekers to remain struggling in a state of imperfection with the hope of some future fulfillment in Heaven after death. Divine Plenitude is fully accessible even here, in the midst of our cultural and personal limitations. The advent of the Messiah, teaches Paul, has fundamentally reoriented human consciousness to this *fullness of Divinity* as its own ground.

This understanding of our intrinsic completeness in the Divine is the gem which, in Paul's language, is freely offered by Grace to faith. What Paul terms faith is the human mood of openness to the revelation of the Christ Nature, not *faith in* some particular set of doctrines, but simply *faith*, free from all efforts at grasping. And as we can see from Paul's own experience of Enlightenment, the mood of faith is itself a gift of Divine Grace, not the fruit of pious human efforts. On the road to Damascus, Paul was not struggling to *believe* the Christian revelation. Illumination dawned spontaneously as Paul let go his conception of orthodoxy, his particular effort to *believe.* We enter this mood of faith when our efforts to grasp or define Divine Nature are suspended. We experience the awareness of what Paul calls *life in Christ* as a gift, which simply means that it is not correlated with any finite efforts or beliefs.

All mystical teaching that reveals the Divine Ground of human nature must face the paradox of our blindness to the Divine or our sense of alienation from the Divine. Human suffering and conflict are created by ignoring our rootedness in the Divine Ground. For this chronic condition of ignorance Paul uses the term *sin*. What Paul calls the Old Aeon is the obscuration of human consciousness by sin. In the New Aeon, sin disappears as mist is burned away by the rising sun, the Grace of Divine Radiance. Paul writes to his disciples in Rome, who have awakened to the mood of faith, *We are dead to sin, so how can we continue to live in it?* This is not an assertion of moral rectitude but a mystical utterance. Those who experience at the core of their being the radiance of Christ Nature live in the New Aeon. Sin, our false sense of separation from the Divine, is the illusion of the Old Aeon, which may appear to persist as a recurrent bad dream but has no actual existence after our *death*, or conscious union with Christ. This mystical union was expressed sacramentally in the early Christian community through the initiation of Baptism. Paul continues: *When we were baptized into union with Christ Jesus we were baptized into his death.* This *death* is the disappearance of the human into the Divine, which attenuates our sense of personal will. After Paul's Baptism in Radiance on the road to Damascus, he no longer willed his actions personally but experienced Christ, or the Divine Nature, willing through him.

These early Christians regarded Baptism not as a rite for children but as an actual experience of transfiguration in which the spiritually mature individual mystically *dies* and *rises*. Explains Paul: *When we were baptized we went into the tomb with him and joined him in death, so that as Christ was raised from the dead by the Father's glory, we too might live a New Life. If in union with Christ we have imitated his death, we shall also imitate him in his resurrection.* The full mystical experience of Baptism in which ordinary water becomes the Fire of Spirit, is reflected in the writings of Zen master Bassui: *Every vestige of self-awareness will disappear and you will feel like a cloudless sky. Within yourself you will find no I . . . even this feeling of voidness will vanish and you will be unaware of everything, total darkness will prevail.* This darkness is the baptism into the death of Jesus, his three days in the tomb. Bassui continues: *If you push forward with your last ounce of strength, and . . . leap with hands up high into the tremendous abyss of fire, into the ever-burning flame of your own primordial nature, all ego-consciousness, all delusive feelings and thoughts and perceptions, will vanish. You will feel resurrected, all sickness having completely vanished, and you will experience genuine peace and joy.* On his way to Damascus, Paul plunged into the fire of the primordial Christ Nature, powerfully transmitted through the early Christians. Thus Paul disappeared into Christ and was resurrected into the New Aeon, or Enlightenment. Ecstatically, he proclaims in a letter to his disciples at Corinth: *For anyone who is in Christ, there is a New Creation; the old creation has gone, and now the new one is here. . . . Such is the richness of the Grace through which God has showered on us all Wisdom and Insight.* This is Enlightenment freely granted not simply to Christian Jews but to all peoples. Through this awakening of the Christ Nature in humanity, the entire universe and its Life is revealed to be of one substance with Godhead, Light from Light, God from God, begotten not made.

The New Aeon pre-exists in the core of the Old Aeon. There is no outer change, simply a new orientation. Reveals Paul: *God has let us know the mystery of His Purpose . . . that He would bring everything together in Christ, everything in the heavens and everything on earth.* Christ is not simply the historical person Jesus, but the principle through which the Godhead manifests as all life. This Christ principle, fully awakened to by Jesus of Nazareth, is revealed by Paul to be the fountainhead of creation, source of the conscious evolutionary energy of life-forms on all planes. As Paul writes: *Christ is the Image of the unseen God . . . for in Christ were created all things in heaven and on earth; everything visible and invisible . . . all things were created through Him and for Him. Before anything was created, He existed, and He holds all things in Unity.* The personal union with Christ which Paul experienced on his way to Damascus has now broadened into the vision of universal unity in Christ on every plane of Being, visible and invisible. What begins as the drama of individual quest and illumination ripens into universal reconciliation or the awakening of all existence to its intrinsic nature as Godhead.

Paul provides a practical human focus in which to anchor the vastness of this vision through his strong emphasis on the community of those living in varying degrees of conscious union with Christ. This mystical *life in Christ* is not for solitary sages but is to be reflected fully in the daily life of an extended spiritual family—men, women, and children who share the consciousness of their unity with the Divine. Paul calls this family the Mystical Body of Christ, and he devoted all his energy to establishing communities that would tangibly represent the Mystical Body throughout the Greek world. His writings are not scholarly or speculative treatises but personal letters to these communities, mediating their internal disputes and strengthening their mystical understanding. Within this extended family there is a rich diversity of viewpoints and gifts, harmonized in the wholeness of the Divine Nature shared fully by all. The members are closer than brothers and sisters. They are functions of a single organism. Explains Paul: *Just as a human body, though it is made up of many parts, is a single unit because all these parts, though many, make one body, so it is with Christ. . . . You together are Christ's Body.* Thus all of us, united with Christ Nature, form one spiritual body, serving individually as limbs and organs for one another. Paul is not speaking metaphorically but from direct spiritual perception of human beings as the Divine Body. This emphasis on community reflects again Paul's richly Jewish orientation. His focus is the extended spiritual family, not the mystically ascending individual soul or the renunciate living in solitude. Yet Paul's communities express all the intensity of commitment and renunciation that are found in the life of the monastery or the solitary hermitage.

The goal of spiritual life in all its forms is that the individual should disappear gracefully into his or her intrinsic nature, which is the Divine Nature. This blending of the separate person into Divine Radiance is accomplished effortlessly if we experience each other to be parts of one Mystical Body, as Paul suggests. Then our sense of separate individuality is attenuated without destroying our special function in the whole. For instance, the hand, although capable of functioning independently, is not a *separate individual.* The organism, the living unity of components, is primary. Although the various limbs and organs are different in useful ways, each expresses exactly the same life. Thus are we to understand the individual members of the Mystical Body of Christ as they express Divine Life.

This Mystical Body is universal, embracing all lives in all galaxies, and is not to be identified with a particular human community or association of communities. Categories of conventional, culture-bound thinking dissolve in this One Body. Exclaims Paul to his disciples in Galatia: *You have all clothed yourselves in Christ, and there are no more distinctions between Jew and Greek, slave and free, male and female.* For an intensely acculturated Jew such as Paul to proclaim no difference between Jew and Greek indicates the ecstatic universalism of the New Aeon that experience of the Christ Nature can generate. There is no fundamental separation between beings in the Mystical Body, which embraces all beings. *Insofar as you did this to one of the least of these brothers of mine, you did it to me,* remarks Jesus, for all beings are the Being that the Christ is and that we are.

Penetrating to the deepest level of the Mystical Body, Paul proclaims: *All of you are One in Christ.* In this dimension of illumination we are no longer envisioned as plural centers of consciousness serving as limbs to each other, but as one Person, one Consciousness, the Self of all selves. To describe this single Consciousness, expressed through transfigured human beings in the New Aeon, Paul uses the term *Spirit.* He remarks: *It is death to limit oneself to what is unspiritual; Life and Peace can come only with concern for the Spirit.* We may understand Spirit as the Ultimate Consciousness in which the transcendent Godhead and the earthly sphere, as well as all intervening planes of Being, are revealed to be the single and perfectly transparent flow of Divine Radiance. On this level of Spirit, the mystic can exist simultaneously as a responsible human being, an ecstatic heavenly being, and as the pure expanse of Godhead beyond all earthly and heavenly forms.

Explains Paul: *Your interests are in the Spirit, since the Spirit of God has made its home in you . . . if Christ is in you, then your Spirit is Life itself.* The spectrum of creation is the radiance of the Divine refracted through Christ Nature, the principle of all conscious life. Spirit is the illumined consciousness of this one Divine Life. Spirit *is* the infinite Divine Life become conscious of Itself, worshiping Itself, creating music through finite instruments. These instruments, which include biological organisms dwelling on planets as well as souls abiding on subtler planes of Being, are not other than the Divine. What appears to our eyes as physical substance and to scientific theory as atoms and electrons is nothing but Divine Radiance, momentarily crystallizing into energy. The Divine alone is. This is why Paul speaks of those who have entered the realm of Spirit as having not only Life but Peace. They have Life because they have awakened to the Divine Life whose radiance is all lives. But since the flow of this Divine Life is dynamic, their Peace is not simply a condition of rest but the perfect release of knowing that the entire play of Being is nothing other than the Divine.

Paul balances this affirmation, that God is all in all, with critical psychological observation appropriate to the Old Aeon. The Old Aeon still appears as what Paul terms our *self-indulgence,* the ignorance, or sin, that proclaims the separate existence of the limited self. The limited self is the dimension of consciousness that has evolved from greed and fear and persists until we can affirm with our whole being that, in Paul's terms, *God is all in all,* that there is nothing to desire or to fear. Even after we begin to live in this illumined affirmation, through mystical Baptism into the New Aeon, the limited self remains as an illusory phantom, reappearing unexpectedly as impulses of greed or fear no longer appropriate on the level of Spirit where there is no fragmentation or separation. This phantom of our limited self must be confronted again and again in spiritual life with the affirmation that God alone is.

Writes Paul: *If you are guided by the Spirit you will be in no danger of self-indulgence, since self-indulgence is the opposite of the Spirit. . . . If you are led by the Spirit, no Law can touch you.* If we enter the realm of Spirit we will be spontaneously pure, harmonious, graceful. There will be neither effort at control nor rationale for control—no Law, as Paul would say. Self-indulgence, or concern for our limited self, springs from the illusion of separateness. As long as we remain ecstatically open at the level of Spirit there is no separation between the self and the Christ Nature. Paul explains, *What the Spirit brings is . . . love, joy, peace, patience, kindness, goodness, trustfulness, gentleness.* These qualities of harmony are what moral codes attempt to instill through various forms of conditioning, but only on the level of Spirit can they arise naturally and sustain themselves without the anxiety and ambition characteristic of the limited self. The morality of the New Aeon is an ecstatic morality based on the disappearance of the human into the Divine, not on the human desire to dominate or control. There can be no prescription of how or how not to act in the Spirit. As Paul writes concerning the harmonious qualities of spiritual life: *There is no Law dealing with such things. . . . Since the Spirit is our life, let us be directed by the Spirit.* Every movement is to be infused by the Spirit through the affirmation that our human nature has disappeared into Divine Nature, that the New Aeon has dawned.

Paul anchors his mystical teaching safely in the tangible daily life of the community. The total freedom of living in the Spirit could be dangerously misinterpreted by the beginner, who needs the example and personal touch of more mature members of the Mystical Body. Ramakrishna used to remark that if one lives among weavers, one will gradually be able to distinguish a forty-one from a forty-two strand thread, simply by touch. Becoming sensitive to the guidance of Spirit is learned from the genuinely ecstatic members of the community, not by rational instruction but as a child learns its own native language. The learning process is gradual, often imperceptible. Although we are no longer intrinsically focused in the limited self, having been baptized into the New Aeon, we fall back again and again into the illusion of self-indulgence, the conventional sense of separation from each other and from the Divine Ground. Paul warns, *Where a man sows, there he reaps: if he sows in the field of self-indulgence he will reap a harvest of corruption.* This is the harvest of disintegration, disharmony, anxiety: the constant suffering and dying which is the life of apparent separation from the Divine. Paul continues: *If one sows in the field of the Spirit, he will reap a harvest of eternal Life.* The eternal is the opposite of the disintegrating. Eternity, which is never frozen, is the integral flow of Divine Life on all planes and beyond all planes. The Peace which we can glimpse as the core of our daily awareness *is* Eternal Life, no less than the life of heavenly beings or the life of the transcendent Godhead. Earth, Heaven, and Godhead share a single essence.

Although attracted by the vision of unity that emerges at what Paul calls the level of Spirit, we may still wonder how to discover a bridge to the ordinary mind, which perceives conflicts and attempts to shape and control situations. Paul's response to this concern can come only from the level of Spirit as a total affirmation of Spirit. What we experience as the perceiving, inquiring, and organizing mind is intrinsically none other than Spirit or Ultimate Consciousness. When the mind is illumined, when its conventional human limits are attenuated, its natural tendency to explore or expand continues. Writes Paul, *These are the things that God has revealed to us through the Spirit, for the Spirit reaches to the depths of everything, even the depths of God.* The spiritually illumined mind which directly perceives its own Divine Ground is not essentially different from that Ground. Reveals Paul, *The depths of God can only be known by the Spirit of God.* Our mind, which is intrinsically Spirit, is none other than God knowing Himself. Our own life is Divine Life. There is no fundamental separation between Divinity and what we call humanity. This is the Messianic revelation by which, in biblical terms, the crooked ways are made straight and the rough places smooth. Our own true nature is the Messiah Nature. As Paul clearly proclaims: *We are those who have the Mind of Christ*. This Divine Mind, which is awakened by our Baptism into the New Aeon, functions also through the ordinary mind. Divine Mind is not separate from any mode of our consciousness. Affirming this truth, daily decisions and behavior become spontaneously prayerful or guided by Spirit. This guidance need not occur only in ecstatic prayer or deep contemplation, because even our ordinary mind, with all its mundane concerns, can transmit as the Mind of Christ.

Awakening to the true nature of our mind brings about the spiritual transfiguration that some cultures call Enlightenment. As Paul writes: *If the administering of the Law, in the written letters engraved on stones, was accompanied by such a brightness that the Israelites could not bear looking at the face of Moses . . . then how much greater is the brightness that surrounds the administering of the Spirit! . . . Where the Spirit is, there is freedom. And we, with our unveiled faces reflecting like mirrors the brightness of the Lord, all grow brighter and brighter as we are turned into the image that we reflect*. The same Transfiguration that occurred to Jesus when he dissolved in Light before the eyes of a few disciples occurs just as significantly to all those who live in union with Christ through Grace. Not only specially evolved souls but all recipients of Grace were known in the New Testament as *saints*. Everyone awakened by the Spirit into the holy community, or Mystical Body, experiences Transfiguration. The full significance and extent of our Transfiguration may dawn only slowly on the ordinary mind, still obscured by traces of the limited self. Transfiguration may be recognized fully only at the moment of death or during the period of spiritual evolution that follows physical death. But there is no reason to wait. When the roots of the limited self have been burned by Baptism in the fire of Spirit,

Transfiguration, or Resurrection, is already occurring. Yet Paul's language cannot be understood by one who has not entered the mood of faith. Ecstatic openness to the Spirit must be granted us by the Spirit perhaps through the very medium of Paul's words. Before our spiritual awakening, these words affirming the arrival of the New Aeon can appear only as pious metaphor or even as madness. Writes Paul: *We teach, not in the way philosophy is taught, but in the may that the Spirit teaches us: we teach spiritual things spiritually. An unspiritual person is one who does not accept anything of the Spirit of God: he sees it all as nonsense; it is beyond his understanding because it can only be understood by means of the Spirit.*

In the New Aeon, the secret of our Divine Life can be proclaimed to all members of all cultures, rather than communicated secretly from the sage to a few disciples. Writes Paul, *It is Christ whom we proclaim. We instruct everyone without distinction in the way of Wisdom.* Swami Vivekananda complained that the Upanishadic wisdom teaching of *Atman*, our intrinsic nature as Ultimate Consciousness, had been restricted in India to small circles of advanced seekers. *You are all pure Spirit, Divine Consciousness*, Vivekananda would proclaim to American audiences at the turn of the nineteenth century. It was with similar bold universality that Paul proclaimed to *everyone without distinction* the mystical union with Christ, the intrinsic Christ Nature of all beings, the dawning of the New Aeon. As Vivekananda dropped certain restrictions of Hindu religious culture in order to communicate its highest wisdom to the Western world, Paul proclaimed freedom from the Jewish Law while communicating to all cultures the deepest promise of Jewish prophetic tradition, the Messianic dawning of the Kingdom of God on earth. In this way, an ancient spiritual tradition universalizes itself through the all-embracing ecstasy of an illumined sage such as Paul or Vivekananda. And Paul's realization of the Christ Nature can continue to serve this process of universalization. As Paul perceived in the radiance of Spirit *no more distinctions between Jew and Greek, slave and free, male and female*, neither can we perceive any fundamental distinction between Jew and Christian, Hindu and Buddhist, theist and nontheist, believer and nonbeliever. There is only one inclusive spiritual family, the Mystical Body, the secret of Divine Life lived fully through the planetary life of conscious beings. Awakening to this secret, instantly we enter the New Aeon.

ALLAH ALONE CAN KNOW ALLAH

Teachings of the Contemporary Sufi Bawa Muhaiyaddeen

Bawa Muhaiyaddeen is a contemporary sage who teaches with compelling power the formless resplendence of Allah and the mystical path which he calls the way of Divine Luminous Wisdom. He emerged from the jungles of Sri Lanka early in our century to teach the simple village people. Now this ageless Sufi master has established a community in Philadelphia, where he travels regularly from India, transmitting mystical Islam to Western culture.

Bawa insists that the Divine cannot be fully understood through the doctrines of any world religion, although he suggests that Islam, with its emphasis on the nature of Allah as utterly formless and transcendent, provides the clearest approach. However, Bawa would not characterize himself simply as Muslim. He teaches that the seeker of God must eventually depart from all religious traditions, which he sees as primarily human institutions. The realm of Divine Resplendence, beyond religion and culture, Bawa calls *open space*. To reach this *open space*, he teaches a harmony of the archetypal ways of wisdom and devotion. His sword of wisdom mercilessly cuts any emotional or conceptual cords that tie us to finite, culture-bound experience. At the same time, our love for God and God's love for His children remain central to Bawa's way.

As we touched the mystical core of Christianity through the letters of Saint Paul, we can glimpse the mystical heart of Islam by reading from a long letter that Bawa wrote me recently from Sri Lanka. He begins, as always, with a prayer: *Allah, may You protect us. May the One God come and hold us in His Hands. May You open our Hearts. May You always exist in our Hearts as the Only One. Ameen.* These words evoke the ultimate wisdom which knows that the Divine is the Only One, that Divine Resplendence alone exists. And yet the form of expression is tender, devotional prayer. Bawa always maintains this delicate balance of wisdom and devotion.

The letter moves to personal greeting, which conveys the blessings and protection of the Divine Power, not just figuratively but with the assurance of someone who actually experiences mystical union with that Power. *May Allah protect you, your wife, your children and all your brothers and sisters. Allah is the Completeness which does not diminish, the Perfection which exists without birth or death, without form, which is endless and cannot be destroyed. May God, as the Mightiest Treasure, protect you, little brother, and give you Grace. May He give you, your wife and children His words of Grace and the Wisdom of Jnana.* Jnana is the Sanskrit term for Gnosis, the liberating knowledge that frees us from all the complications of the created universe by revealing our kinship with the formless Source of creation, by revealing our soul's intrinsic transcendence of the universe. Bawa moves easily between the mystical terminologies of Tamil, Sanskrit, and Arabic. Before becoming a spiritual teacher, he wandered for decades throughout India, China, and the Middle East, observing the religious practices of these cultures with the Jnana, or Divine Luminous Wisdom, which experiences Divine Power as formless, transcendent, and inexpressible.

The letter continues: *May He who is existing as the Father of Wisdom in the heavenly worlds give you Wisdom, or Jnana, and may He give you a palace of Grace in the heaven of Jnana. May He protect you. Ameen. My love to you, your wife, and your children, and to God's children who are joined with you, my little brother. I offer all of you the Love of my heart. I offer my love and salaams to those who exist as the Heart within my heart. I offer love to you, my little brother who is in the form of Love.* Bawa regards spiritual seekers as expressions of the Divine Heart hidden within the human heart, as essentially expressions of God. As Saint Paul teaches, we come to know God by the movement through us of God's own Holy Spirit. Bawa shares this attitude and reminds us continually that in his words, *only Allah can know Allah.* And it is only God who seeks God. The spiritual longing that expresses itself through human beings is none other than the Divine Power circling into Itself. Bawa's intense love for seekers is simply his love for God. Bawa also shares with Saint Paul the teaching of Divine Grace, which is not usually prominent in the path of wisdom. When Bawa prays for *a palace of Grace in the heaven of Jnana,* he is suggesting that Gnosis, or liberating knowledge, does not originate from the seeker through human effort but is received as a priceless gift from the Divine.

Bawa speaks of the seeker as existing *in the form of Love.* Here he is evoking the essence of Islamic mystical thought. Although Allah is perfectly formless Divine Power, He is not without attributes such as Justice, Compassion, Wisdom, and Love. Although the Divine Power is never considered in Islam to assume human form, human beings can fully participate in these Divine Attributes. In fact, the principle of humanity is none other than the progressively clearer manifestation of the Divine Attributes. The Wisdom within human wisdom and the Love within human love are fully Divine. Bawa mystically perceives himself and all seekers of God *in the form of Love,* in no way separate from God's own quality of Love. Yet Bawa often introduces his discourses with the remark, *I am no more significant than an ant.* With this use of the pronoun *I,* Bawa refers to his human organism, which is simply another dimension of the created universe and remains quite distinct from the Divine Wisdom and Love that focus through this organism. For Bawa, Divine Power focuses through the world but can never be identified with the world or any of its creatures.

His letter continues: *Little brother, since I have come back to Ceylon I have not had time to write letters. There is so much work in the world, there is so much work to do for the creations of God. I have to stop disease and calm minds. I have to be in the form of Love to do this. I have to cool and calm their hearts and give them happiness. I do not have time to write you a pen or pencil letter. I wrote you a letter which was as the Heart within your heart, as Wisdom within wisdom, little brother. It is in your pure heart that I wrote a letter; maybe you can understand this.* Through powerful daily discourses, which last several hours, Bawa clarifies the nature of the universe and the Divine Power, thus bringing peace to the agitated minds of seekers. His words have an equally calming effect among those with no formal education and those with years of university training.

Each day, Bawa also works to heal diseased bodies and minds. I once watched him observe a young woman who was addicted to tranquilizers and medicinal drugs. He looked at his own hand. One of his disciples later told me that he reads information psychically from the palm of his own hand as from a vast computer. Bawa remarked to this young woman, *I have examined every nerve in your body, and they are all subtly destroyed by these drugs. They have been burned, as if scorched by fire. You have taken six different types of drugs. And you have pain in certain parts of your body.* As he told her the details, she confirmed the diagnosis.

Bawa has access to other psychic or spiritual powers which have been used beneficially by authentic shamans in all cultures. When I saw Bawa last, he remarked, *Little brother, last night I came to visit you, early in the morning when your family were all asleep.* I silently wondered why Bawa would take the trouble to project his awareness from Philadelphia to New York, and he immediately replied: *You know, it really is not difficult. The entire world is like the point of an atom. You think it is such a big place. It is really very insignificant, like a tiny seed. It is not hard to go about and visit people.* We assume that our ordinary experience of spatial and temporal extension is an accurate perception of reality, just as we assume that matter is solid. Authentic masters of Consciousness such as Bawa enable us to form more accurate notions about the nature of energy and mind. Yet Bawa, for all his powers and understanding, never claims perfection or Enlightenment. He always includes himself among the seekers of God. As he writes, *Little brother, your wife and children and I have to know what the reason for this world is.* His humility is not rhetorical but spontaneous, an expression of continual worship or contemplation of Allah as the only reservoir of Wisdom and Power. I once started to ask Bawa about his own state of illumination, but he interjected, even before I had finished posing the question, *I do not know, I do not know, I am still learning. I have much work to do, I am still studying.* He is an eternal student of the Divine, completely suffused by the Divine.

Bawa expresses a complex attitude toward this created universe in which the transcendental human soul finds itself temporarily focused. He regards the realm of physical and mental energy as dangerously seductive and fundamentally alien to the nature of the soul, which is a ray shining directly from the Divine. Yet he also recognizes this universe as a school designed carefully by the Divine for the soul's education. In the first mood, Bawa implies that the soul should sever its relationship with an alien universe. In the second mood, he suggests that Divine Wisdom and Power is beautifully expressed through creation and that the soul can benefit from the observation and study of all phenomena. These two moods, as we will see, are not actually contradictory, yet their interplay can be confusing.

As Bawa's letter continues, he expresses in the first of these moods the urgent sense that what he calls *the world of mind and desire* is like a forest on fire from which we should escape immediately. *When what we see is changed, when our hands change, when what we see is destroyed, when our food is gone, then this body will be destroyed. Sleep will be gone then and the world will be destroyed. Wasting the daylight in your heart is not good.* Because of his Islamic orientation, Bawa does not think in terms of gradual spiritual evolution of the soul through a series of incarnations. He regards most human beings as souls in their first and potentially last incarnation in this school of physical embodiment. His emphasis is on the liberation of the soul from the world, and he considers a single lifetime sufficient for the dawning within any soul of the Gnosis, or Divine Luminous Wisdom, which is already its intrinsic nature. Bawa accepts the process of reincarnation, but departs from the traditional interpretation of this doctrine by suggesting that the soul has most immediate access to the Divine in its first lifetime and this access becomes less easy as the soul reincarnates again and again.

This is contrary to the view of Hindu and Buddhist sages. Such sharp disagreement between illumined saints and sages from various cultural backgrounds concerning the structures and functions of relative existence will not disappear. The unavoidable factor of cultural and personal perspective makes full agreement about the nature of earthly and heavenly existence impossible. Yet Godhead, or Ultimate Reality, is essentially without structure or function, and there is fundamental agreement among mystics on this ultimate level. On this level, Bawa recognizes that there is only the formless Power which he calls Allah and that the world as a university for souls is simply a mirage or play within the Divine.

Bawa suggests that all objects and structures are projected by mind and exist only for the collective mind of sentient beings. He presents this insight by pointing out the essential similarity between waking and dream, a similarity that is not simply metaphorical but reflects the fundamental nature of all phenomena as Consciousness. The only difference between waking and dreaming is that the waking state constitutes a collective dream, continually renegotiated and roughly agreed upon by all conscious beings, whereas the dream state is subjective, or private to each individual center of consciousness. Bawa begins by describing subjective dream: *This is what we have to think about and understand, little brother. Our intentions become like vows, our vows become like ideas, our ideas become like sleep and our sleep turns into dreams. These are the dreams seen in the time of darkness.* He then extends this analysis of subjective dream to the realm of collective, or waking, dream: *Desire becomes lust, lust becomes delusion, delusion becomes the mind, the mind becomes dark, glitters come in the darkness as the appearance of mental visions. Mental visions become the world, the world becomes men, the men become actors. This act becomes a man's life. Man's life becomes an act which he is acting. This act is the daydream. This is the dream seen in the day.* Sleeping dream and waking dream are not fundamentally different: they both exist as mental projection. And yet Bawa counsels us to take the waking dream seriously: to be careful with all lives, to regard all suffering as our own, and to observe precisely all phenomena, tracing them to their ultimate source in Allah. Thus we learn to manifest more and more clearly the attributes of God such as Justice, Compassion, and Wisdom. Our learning to become transparent to the Divine, expressing more and more clearly the Divine Attributes, is the purpose of this collective dream we call the universe and which is actually, as Bawa elsewhere reveals, God dreaming through us.

Bawa now evokes the Gnosis, or liberating insight with which we can see through this Cosmic Dream. *This is the world, little brother. The state of this world is what we have to see and think about with Wisdom. We must see without thought, without dreams, without night, without day, without happiness or sadness, without forms or statues, without end or destruction, without beginning or birth, without selfishness, without pride, without hunger, without old age, without disease, without death, without anger, without intoxicants, without lust, without theft, without lies, without arrogance, without karma, without illusion, without ignorance, without hurry, without race, without religion, without blood ties, without mantras, without showing miracles, without titles, without fame.* Yet this Wisdom which moves by negation is not, for Bawa, a total *via negativa*, as in some wisdom teachings. It does not eliminate the positive attributes of Allah, such as Justice and Compassion. These beneficent qualities of God can be named in human language because they are originally revealed and transmitted by Divine Grace through the spiritually awakened human being who shares with Allah His *form of Love.* As Bawa explains: *The highest Treasure, Allah, is in the form of pure Love, existing with three thousand compassionate and beneficent qualities, existing as Love within love, embracing each life with patience, restraint, contentment, surrender, tolerance, peacefulness and the qualities which exist as the calming honey of Grace.*

Entering ecstasy, Bawa now reveals that God and the Divine Attributes alone truly exist, that both subjective dreams and the Cosmic Dream are ultimately unreal, appearing only provisionally as a teaching for souls: *O God, there is no one else. There is none other than He. All the rest, all the other things are ideas and dreams. Dreams in the night and dreams seen in the day are what these things are. This is what we have to think about, little brother.* Bawa speaks about the manifest, or dreamed, universe as God's Story. This endlessly complicated Story exists for beings to study it, but the ultimate goal of studying this dream tale is simply to awaken from it, not to catalogue its infinite patterns and details. This awakening Bawa describes as a return to our *original form.* As his letter continues: *The dreams seen at night and the dreams seen during the day are the actors. But they will have to end their acts, they will have to take off their make-up and some day show their true forms. Then they will know their original form.* All forms are masks of God. All sentient beings express the pure Consciousness and Power that is Allah. When they remove their masks, they will know their *original form,* which is, paradoxically, without form or structure.

Bawa playfully describes our human situation thus: *The earthly world is a stage. The mind of man is the world. Desire and the monkey mind are the actors. These actors can only act in the darkness. When we turn on the house lights, their glitter, their make-up and their act will be finished. Little brother, we must put on this light. We must wire our heart and put in the bulb so we can become resplendent. You and I, little brother, and all these children must do this and see with this resplendent light of Divine Luminous Wisdom. Wherever there is illusion, darkness, magic, we have to switch on the light. We must not think about what happened before this, we must understand what is happening now. We have to take one point from all this. We have to know our Father.* Setting aside the infinitely involved Story of the manifest universe, we are to concentrate on its essence, which is the Resplendence of Allah, the Divine Father. From this Resplendence alone the entire Cosmic Dream is woven. But again and again, in the masculine metaphor characteristic of Bible and Koran, Bawa speaks of the Divine as *Father.* Allah is not for Bawa, an impersonal Reality. Even in God's ultimate nature as pure Light and Power there still exist the fatherly or motherly qualities of Wisdom and Love.

From the language of wisdom, Bawa now modulates to the language of devotion. *We must see our Father. He created us, and He gives us food. He protects us. He nourishes us with the Honey of the Milk of His Grace. The explanation comes from His Holy Mouth.* Bawa participates as fully in the way of devotion as in the way of wisdom. He accepts both the fatherly creator God and the absolute Resplendence for which there is neither creation nor destruction. Bawa never implies that the Divine Father who protects and nourishes His children is any less ultimate than the transcendent Godhead which knows no play of creation. For the mystical union, which Bawa describes as *knowing the Father* or *returning to the Father,* he evokes both liberating knowledge and ecstatic love.

Bawa's letter returns again to the language of Gnosis, describing the process that separates the dross of relative existence from the gold of Divine Resplendence. *We have to wash and separate everything with the acid of Wisdom. Other than Allah, the pure Treasure, everything else will be dissolved. Allah is the only Treasure which cannot be destroyed. My dear little brother, who is like a gem within my eye, it is like that. Do not worry if all the rest goes. There is only One. The brass, the copper, the nickel and the other alloys will be dissolved and the pure gold will remain. That is Allah. We must not think of all other alloys, which will melt away. This Treasure which cannot be burned away is One. All others will go. That One will remain when the acid of Wisdom is applied. You do this and see. This will be good.* Bawa is suggesting here the perfect disappearance of the human into the Divine, the ultimate spiritual surrender or renunciation to which the saints of all cultures aspire. Yet he speaks of this sublime and arduous process so simply and naturally that it appears attainable even by the ordinary seeker of God.

What lies behind this encouraging attitude is Bawa's unbounded reverence for every human soul as a ray from Allah. Were we merely organic creatures, application of the Wisdom which dissolves all creation would be impossible, but what Bawa terms *the original birth of Man* transcends the cosmos. Explains Bawa: *There are so many millions of births which exist in this world. But there is something above them all. This is the beautiful pure birth, the Original Birth of Man.* Bawa uses the term *Man* as an esoteric or secret word for the Divine. *Man* is not a certain species on a particular planet, but Divine Power projecting Its own Image. Wherever this Divine Image appears, focused through the evolutionary process on any suitable planet, the result is *Man,* in the esoteric meaning of the term, regardless of the particular physical organism involved. Bawa often remarks laconically, *Man-God God-Man,* suggesting the secret equivalence in essence between Divinity and humanity, as between the sun and its rays. One thinks of Allah in the context of strict Islamic monotheism as wholly other than mankind. But this complete separation between Man and God is not borne out by Islamic mystical experience. In Sufi language, the human lover is mysteriously inseparable from the Divine Beloved. Evoking the transcendent nature of Man, Bawa continues: *Other than this birth of Man there are many beasts, reptiles, birds, insects, the sun, moon and the stars, water, fire, earth, air, ether, trees, plants. So many millions have come and been born and live in this world, but the birth of Man is beyond. All the rest are born and will change.* The vision of this transcendent and eternal Humanity is to be clearly distinguished from any pantheism which regards human beings as Divine. No form can be Divine, teaches Bawa, for Allah is utterly without form.

Human imagination tends to romanticize the natural order of being, whereas the mystical path of transcendence reverses this tendency by cultivating critical detachment from the created universe. While he stresses that ultimately only Allah exists, Bawa maintains a strong negative dialectic which refuses to reverence the world and its creatures as Divine. Ramakrishna tells a suggestive parable about the paradoxical relation between the negative dialectic, or path of transcendence, and the mystical experience of Divine omnipresence. When we climb steps to the roof, with each step we think, *This is not the roof,* yet when we finally reach the roof, we discover it to be composed of the same brick as the steps. However, had we not engaged in negative dialectic or denial at each step, we might never have reached the roof. When we reach the *roof,* or mystical union, we will perceive all dimensions of the created universe, or *steps,* as expressions of the same Divine Power. Then we will know that the Divine alone exists, that Allah alone can know Allah. But we must never remain captivated by the beauty or apparent completeness of any particular *step* along the ascent.

Bawa explains: *The One born as Man must know who He is. The earth, fire, air, water, ether and their various aspects must be seen and known. Then there is the Light of the Soul. Discard all the rest and see It.* This sharp discrimination between the soul on the one hand and the physical, biological, and psychological realms on the other, Bawa shares with certain philosophers of India. These thinkers strictly discriminate the principle of Consciousness, Soul or *Purusha,* from the material principle, *prakriti,* the manifestations of nature that Bawa identifies as earth, fire, air, water, ether, and their infinite permutations. Soul, or pure Consciousness, is perceived by this dualistic Indian metaphysics as intrinsically unconnected with nature, which is simply matter in motion. Sense perception, as well as thinking that is related to the senses, are regarded by these philosophers of the yogic school as merely a process of subtle material change, not a function of Purusha, or Soul. But Bawa transmutes this intense dualism through his ultimate understanding that the Divine Power alone exists. From his perspective, the play of the five elements becomes God's Dream or Story rather than the independent activity of some material principle separate from or opposed to the Divine.

However, Bawa is reticent about the secret teaching that Allah alone exists. I once asked him how the five elements could possibly be *other than* the Power and Resplendence of Allah, which is all-encompassing. Bawa avoided any direct answer, preferring that the puzzle's solution, that Allah alone is, be experienced directly for myself. The reason for this reticence is made plain by Ramakrishna's parable of climbing the steps. It is not conducive to spiritual growth to remain on a lower step and speculate whether the roof is an expression of the same Divine Power as the step is. We must generate the strength and discipline actually to ascend the steps, reach the roof, and eventually understand for ourselves that the Divine alone exists both as immanence and transcendence, as the *steps* and the *roof*. Bawa and other illumined teachers employ the negative dialectic, *this is not God, that is not God,* simply as an effective means to give transcendent direction and impetus to our spiritual practice. They know that ultimately God alone is.

We must remember, however, that Bawa's teaching is not an abstract metaphysics which in any way ignores earthly reality. His attitude toward the Divine Dream which appears as the universe of matter in motion is not one of rejection. He counsels spiritual students to observe every phenomenon with utmost care and precision. Bawa himself became an expert in herbal medicine during the long years of his seclusion in the jungles of Ceylon, and applies in all matters the attitude of a scientific investigator. It was this relentless attitude of observation and analysis which enabled Bawa to penetrate through phenomena and past traditional religious forms to the *open space* of Enlightenment. This intense aliveness of observation and investigation eventually reveals itself as what Bawa terms Divine Luminous Wisdom, the primordial nature of God and Man.

Bawa's letter continues: *The treasure which has come from Allah is the Soul or the Ray. That is the Light. When you discover and trace that Light, the rays which come from it will disappear into that Treasure. That Light is Man. It is not this body. This is the Treasure we have to receive.* This tracing of the ray which is our primal awareness, or soul, back to its source in Ultimate Consciousness, or Allah, is for Bawa a process of simultaneous Love and Wisdom. Bawa regards this return along the ray of soul into Transcendence as the essence of all worship and contemplation. He expresses a critical attitude toward any practice of ritualistic worship or any meditative technique which has lost sight of this essence. Bawa is intensely critical about the tendency of religious traditions to replace worship and contemplation of the transcendent Divine with obeisance to authority symbols, whether persons or doctrines. This he calls *becoming slaves to others.*

In this critical vein, Bawa's letter continues: *We have to understand this, little brother, all this becoming slaves to others, all this searching and running. The body sings and dances and becomes a slave to others, but we must pray to Allah alone. There are no mantras, no tricks, no magics, no religions, no creeds for meditation. God has to worship God. The Soul has to worship the Soul. Light has to worship Light. There is only One for meditation.* There is no need to run in search of God, clinging to religions or creeds, because Divine Resplendence cannot be contained by finite modes of worship or patterns of belief. It is only the Divine who can truly worship the Divine, using the human soul as Its medium of expression. Bawa does not encourage the conventional practice of any religious tradition. Although his imagery and approach are drawn from Islam,

Bawa tirelessly asserts that Allah is the formless Power which abides in the *open space* beyond all religions. Bawa, like any authentically illumined being, is not definable religiously or culturally. He has no role. He is simply God worshiping God.

Bawa continues: *Those who are racists, those who have connections with religions, the people who are tied by bonds of blood and kinship, these are the ones who will be carried to the cemetery. This is the world, little brother. Allah is One. He has no body, no death, no birth, no beginning, no end, no want, no form, no status. He is not the light as we see it. He is not the sun, the moon, the stars, the fire, or the glitters. He is always pure. He is omnipresent Perfection. He exists as the Atom within the atom, as the Heart within the heart, as Wisdom within wisdom.* Such phrases as *the Atom within the atom* suggest the omnipresence of the Divine while avoiding the identification of the Divine with finite existence. Human intelligence, for instance, is a reflection of the Divine in the finite world of mind and desire, but the essence of this intelligence, *the Intelligence within the intelligence,* as Bawa would say, is the very Divine Consciousness which projects this universe. The Heart within our human heart is God's infinite Love, the Atom within the physical atom is the eternal Divine Power. The Dream within our infinitely various dreams is God's Dream.

This Story, or Dream, is our path to its Source, the Resplendence of Allah. As we advance along this path, we hear Divine Resonance. For the Sufi practitioner, this primal Divine Sound can be experienced through the subtle and sacred vibration of the Arabic word *Allah-Hu,* but it is essentially beyond language and culture. Continues Bawa: *Allah is the Heart within the heart, the Wisdom within wisdom. The Light of Allah is the most high purity. And Allah-Hu is the Resonance of Allah. That, little brother, is our most precious and perfect Treasure. What has to be known within our wisdom is this Resonance.* Constant awareness of this mystic Sound is the contemplative practice into which Bawa initiates his spiritual children. He does not regard this as a meditation technique, like the repetition of a mantra, but as listening to the Resonance of God, which is always occurring. As *Allah-Hu suggests the meaning, in Arabic, Allah only*, it evokes the ultimate insight that the Divine alone exists. The *Allah-Hu* is attuned to with each breath, day and night, until breathing becomes not only a natural remembrance of Allah but a conscious emanation of Divine Presence. Bawa does not counsel his disciples to withdraw for a certain period each day to practice meditation: the Breath within each breath is the Resonance of God. We are to discover *Allah-Hu* rather than practice it. Who other than God is there to practice the contemplation that God alone exists? In Bawa's words: *it is Allah who must worship Allah.*

Bawa counsels us to merge our breath with this Holy Breath, to ground all our thinking there, and in that sense, as Bawa says, *to think of nothing else.* As his letter continues: *Little brother, you and I, your wife, your children, all our brothers and sisters have to search for and merge with this Treasure. We must not think of anything else. Allah is the only One. His Grace is always within our hearts. May we accept and know only Him. May we accept and receive Him. All Praise and all Love belong to Allah. Allah is the only One. All Splendor belongs to Him. He is the Secret within our lives.* Allah projects Himself secretly yet fully through human beings within the mirage of manifestation in order to return to Himself continuously. This mystic return is not our personal struggle but simply God's meditation, which breathes out as manifest Being and breathes in as the path of Love and Wisdom. This is the endless play of Divine Power, the Resonance of *Allah-Hu*, or *God only.*

As we move toward the liberating experience of *God only*, however, we must intensify our realistic and critical evaluation of the human dilemma, the absurdity and selfishness of conventional life in what Bawa humorously calls *the A, B, C, D world.* In less playful moods, Bawa refers to human ruthlessness and deception as the realm of hell and sin, whether it occurs in the context of planetary life or on more subtle planes of existence, where the power of the psyche is enhanced by the disappearance of physical limitations. That the torture and suffering of war, for instance, can be perpetrated in the name of political or religious systems, grounded in economic interest or the will to dominate, confirms the *sinful* nature of what Bawa calls *mind and desire*. During wartime, however, one also encounters intensified expressions of sacrifice, tenderness, loyalty. These are reflections of the Divine Love and Wisdom which are focusing through the human being. Sin is not intrinsic to our nature, according to Bawa, as we are fundamentally expressions of the Divine Attributes. But to attune to our soul, which is a ray from Allah, we must consciously discard the *sinful* and therefore *hellish* dimension of personal and collective experience.

Bawa continues: *Little brother, all of us must discard this body of hell which exists as sin, we must discard this birth in hell which exists as sin. We must be given the Resplendent Body of Grace, we must be given the Beauty of Light. We must be given the Love, the Compassion and the Grace belonging to the Father of Divine Wisdom. May He take us into His Hands and embrace us. May He nourish us with His Milk of Grace, with His Honey of Grace.* Divine Grace is the secret of spiritual awakening. Since the realm of sin is created by the fanatic human striving to attain whatever is desired, further striving, even in the name of religion, cannot free us from sin. Grace is experienced as a gift because it is already there, quite apart from any effort at grasping or controlling, when we turn to our intrinsic nature, or soul. Grace is the spontaneous affirmation that God alone exists, the Resonance of *Allah-Hu*. This primal affirmation or Divine Resonance *is* our soul. Enlightenment is the awakening to our intrinsic nature, or soul, and Grace is the only way this can occur. There is nothing *we* could possibly *do*, for there is neither *we* nor *doing* apart from the Divine. We do not give ourselves to Allah but are offered to Allah by Allah. Authentic spiritual life is simply the play of the Divine with Itself, not any process of human access to the Divine. For Bawa, no religion can purvey access to the Divine. God is never bought or sold in the religious marketplace. There is, in the ultimate sense, no access to the Divine, for there is no real existence apart from the Divine which could seek this access, and the Divine needs no access to Itself.

As Bawa explains: *He is the only One. There is nothing we can give Him, for He is the only One. He is the One who gives. God is not someone who accepts or likes our things. He is the One who is Generous. He gives everything. He is the Ruler of immeasurable Grace. This Power has no possessions. He exists as His own Possession. His Story can be known through all of His creations. His creations have His Story within them. This is what we have to know and understand. The place in which this is understood is called Man.* We are to understand the essence of God's Story, not its infinite detail. The essence is that the Divine alone is. Bawa calls this Truth. *There is one Truth which we have to know in our lives. That one Truth is undiminishing, incomparable, indestructible, beginningless, endless, without sorrow. It is the Perfect Purity which exists every second.*

There is no concept or doctrine which touches this Truth. The fundamental theme of Bawa's teaching is that Allah is inexpressible by the human mind. However, Allah touches and expresses Himself through the human soul, which is a ray of His Power. This is the play of the Divine with Itself, not a religious system designed by mind and desire, the mind and desire which Bawa calls maya, or mirage. As Bawa's letter continues: *Allah can be touched with His Power, and that Power exists as a point in the Heart of Man. There is one Church or Temple there. That Power in which God exists is His Temple. This Temple cannot be found with any kind of instrument. It cannot be found with anything which has a relationship to the earth. It cannot be picked up or found with any of the four quadrillion magnetic powers of the magnet of maya. It cannot be seen. It is the Treasure which transcends and stays beyond mind and desire. God has built that Temple with His Grace. As He created, God placed a Temple within each heart in which He can be worshiped and prayed to. He has built that Mosque in the Heart of Man. It has not been built with the earth. It has not been built with anything connected* to the earth. *That is the Temple in which His Presence can be found and where Allah can be prayed to.* Since this Divine Power has no connections, It leaves no traces. Various techniques of concentration and the psychic experiences they produce also cannot pick up or tune in this Power but perceive only echoes or reflections of Divine Power in the complex realm of mind and desire. Enlightenment simply *is* that Power, not any doctrinal or ritual attempt to pick It up, organize It, and appropriate It for human use. That Power is the spontaneous Grace of the *Allah-Hu,* the ecstatic affirmation that Allah alone is, which emanates directly from God. Man, or Soul, is the affirmation that God alone is.

Bawa tirelessly reveals the Truth that Allah alone exists, that Allah alone is worshiping Allah through this Dream or Story that we experience as the universe. *Allah is a Pauper to a pauper. He is a Rich Man to a rich man. He is a Learned Man to a learned man. He is a King to a king. He is a Poet to a poet. He is a Knower of Truth to a knower of truth. Allah worships those who worship Him.* Allah is the inner core of all beings: He is the Rich Man within the rich man, the Pauper within the pauper, the Divine Power behind all masks. That *Allah worships those who worship Him* suggests that the worshipers of the Divine are themselves the Divine, for Allah worships only Allah. Bawa's attitude toward seekers is that they are fundamentally expressions of the Divine. When Bawa tenderly embraces each seeker, as he does after every discourse, it is only God embracing God. This embrace is the affirmation that God alone is.

Bawa's long letter ends with a blessing through which he embraces all of us who are now reading his words, invoking for us what he calls the *direct path* which reveals our life as the worship of Allah by Allah. *Little brother, I understand your love, your heart, your wisdom, your efforts, and your faith in God. May Allah give you, your wife, your children the most exalted Grace. May He give you His Wealth of Grace and His Perfection. Ameen. May He open the hearts of all the children who are joined with us. May He show all of them the Direct Path. May He take everyone to the Shore and give all of them His Light of Grace. Ameen.* Following this Direct Path, we discover ourselves to be Allah in the form of Love. As Bawa ecstatically prays: *Oh, One who is in the form of Love! Oh, our own form of Love! Keep us within your Love, give us your Grace, and protect all of us. Ameen. Ya Rabeel Alameen.*

CHAPTER NINE

CONVERSATION WITH AN ANCIENT CHINESE SAGE

[handwritten: Confucious]
[handwritten: Lao-tzu (TAOIST)]

The Oracle Text of the I Ching

The *Book of Changes* is a Chinese oracle text which, when consulted reverently, can be experienced as a sensitive spiritual friend. I approached this friend, using the traditional coin ritual, and posed questions about the process of Enlightenment. The oracle's responses blend the Confucian sense of balance with the Taoist appreciation of flow. I record this divination not only to evoke the unique tones of devotion and wisdom that Chinese culture has evolved but also to present an actual experience of revelation in which spiritual guidance was received through the medium of the oracle. This revelatory interlude was intimate and clear.

The poles of living energy we encounter through the hexagrams, or sixty-four basic configurations of the *Book of Changes*, are Yin and Yang. We are not simply observing the statistical possibilities of tossing three coins six times. Through this ritual of divination which focuses what we call *change*, archetypal patterns, rich in symbolic meaning, are revealed. The ancient Chinese sage Lao-tzu described his own spiritual experience of these polar energies of change, Yin and Yang, as a *voyage to Life's beginning*. Tradition ascribes these words to the Taoist master: *I saw Yin, the female energy, in its motionless grandeur. I saw Yang, the male energy, grounded in its fiery vigor. The motionless grandeur came about the earth, the fiery vigor burst out in heaven, the two penetrated one another, were inextricably blended, and from their union the things of the world were born.* When we consult the *Book of Changes*, we should remember, with the venerable Lao-tzu, that we are voyaging into Life's beginning, that we are enabled through the medium of the oracle to observe and understand the universe as it emanates from its Source, or the Tao. This voyage is the process of Enlightenment expressed through Chinese spiritual culture: its Yin the Taoist appreciation of the formless flow of life, its Yang the Confucian concern for the delicate balance of human society.

I began by asking the oracle whether there is harmony among diverse paths of devotion and wisdom. Can spiritual life be understood as a planetary symphony, blending countless cultural instruments? The oracle responded with Hexagram 24: Return or Turning Point. The ancient commentary interprets the pattern of this hexagram: *The idea of a turning point arises from the fact that after the dark lines have pushed all the light lines upward and out of the hexagram, another light line enters the hexagram from below. The time of darkness is past.* This time of darkness is the atmosphere of tension and contradiction among the religious practices and images emerging from contrasting cultures. There is now a *turning point* when the harmony of all ways to Enlightenment can begin to be accepted as a fundamental principle of cultural expression and personal spiritual growth. The judgment of the oracle is: *Return. Success.* This is return to the primal harmony at the beginning of Life, coming home to the primordial dimension where fragmentation or alienation does not occur. Primal harmony is accessible in every sacred tradition and historical era, but a special sense of its accessibility occurs in the atmosphere of a single planetary civilization and in the global awareness which is Enlightenment.

The oracle continues: *Going out and coming in without error. Friends come without blame. To and fro goes the way.* The mood suggested is one free from judgments. The way to Enlightenment is every way. The Taoist experience of intuitive friendship with nature expands into friendship with all languages and images of the spiritual quest. The commentary reads: *There is movement but it is not brought about by force.* The mood of harmony creates a spiritual movement which is spontaneous. During the *time of darkness,* when various modes of worship and understanding exist in mutual tension and even conflict, force is exerted on individuals to bring them along one particular ritual or doctrinal path to the exclusion of all others. There is the spiritual force exerted by miraculous powers and events, the psychic force generated by strong individual personalities or by group pressure, and the political force by which governments impose creeds on people under their power. By contrast, the dawning of harmony, in the words of the oracle, *is not brought about by force.* The mood of harmony seeks to confine no one. Each person is allowed to return or to come home along his or her own way, and these interrelated ways are now perceived as complementary.

The commentary on the oracle continues: *The lower trigram is characterized by devotion. Thus the movement is natural, arising spontaneously.* This dawning of harmony among spiritual paths is characterized by devotion, love, intuitive sympathy. The sword of liberating knowledge may be used to cut through the confusion of various religious sects, dissolving doctrines and rituals in the vision of Ultimate Reality. But the healing of tensions and the harmonizing of various paths to Enlightenment cannot be brought about by force, not even by the subtle force of liberating knowledge. The oracle recommends the spiritual nonviolence of the Taoist Way, which gracefully makes friends with all forms of life, planting in the rich soil of devotion, tenderly nurturing rather than seeking to dominate. All beings are thus regarded as growing from the same soil, distinct from each other as herbs, vegetables, and flowers, yet fundamentally in harmony.

Yet this attitude of sympathy or love is characterized by a

clarity free from the culture-bound emotions often associated with religious devotion. Blind devotion to certain rituals or doctrines is the cause of the sectarian conflict, the time of darkness, that is dispelled by the return to primal harmony. The oracle describes the practical manner in which this vision can manifest: *Societies of people sharing the same views are formed. But since these groups come together in full public knowledge and are in harmony with the time, all selfish separatist tendencies are excluded, and no mistake is made.* This picture contains genuine spiritual diversity. No harmony can imply the suppression of the individual notes that constitute the harmony. The tones of each sacred tradition remain clear and strong, yet *separatist tendencies* disappear.

From the Taoist perspective, this harmony among various ways of being already exists naturally. We are to *return* to natural balance, to perceive all ways as *returning* to the Source. The oracle continues: *The idea of Return is based on the course of nature. The movement is cyclic and the course completes itself. Therefore it is not necessary to hasten anything artificially. Everything comes of itself at the appointed time. This is the meaning of heaven and earth.* Authentic spiritual ripening is seen to come about spontaneously. Taoist nonviolence includes the absence of striving. There is no need to impose pressure on ourselves or on others, for the return to primal harmony, or Enlightenment, *comes of itself at the appointed time.* The oracle suggests that the meditative or prayerful mood appropriate to this Return is a form of rest rather than striving. *Movement is just at its beginning, therefore it must be strengthened by rest, so that it will not be dissipated by being used prematurely.* Specific religious or esoteric practices are no longer envisioned as directly causing spiritual growth. The contemplative mood of rest from striving simply assists the return to harmony which is occurring naturally and inevitably. Reads the oracle: *The return of health after illness, the return of understanding after an estrangement, everything must be treated tenderly and with care at the beginning so that the return may lead to a flowering.* This tenderness is the delicate touch, the Taoist effortlessness and nonviolence, which is appropriate to the New Dawn or Turning Point.

The oracle warns against a particular danger along this way of harmony. Reads the commentary: *There are people of a certain inner instability who feel a constant urge to reverse themselves. There is danger in continually deserting the good because of uncontrolled desires, then turning back to it again because of a better resolution.* An immature lack of resolution and discipline is often expressed by experimenting with one spiritual practice after another. The harmony of all paths does not divest us of the responsibility of commitment, although this commitment no longer need be exclusive or judgmental. The oracle is not severe about the tendency to wander in various directions: *Since this does not lead to habituation in evil, a general inclination to overcome the defect is not wholly excluded.* Freedom to experiment with various religious practices and languages is central to the mood of harmony, although such experimentation can become a subtle diversion from authentic spiritual life. Yet the initial confusion which may arise from a variety of involvements is no more dangerous than zealous or narrow commitment to a single religious tradition. As the oracle expresses this attitude of freedom: *Repeated return. Danger. No blame.*

The ritual toss of coins often indicates a second hexagram, suggesting the direction of movement or development. To my original question, the oracle responded with Turning Point, or Return. We are to come home into the natural, primal harmony which always is. The further direction of development was indicated by Hexagram 63: After Completion. Completion, in this context, may be understood as Enlightenment, the understanding that actually perceives primal harmony in all situations. The commentary on the oracle describes this illumination through the Confucian ideal of delicate balance, or order: *This hexagram is the further evolution of Hexagram 11: Peace. The transition from confusion to order is completed, and everything is in its proper place, even in particulars.* The confusion engendered by accepting all ways as the Tao, or True Way, will gradually evolve into the continuous sense of balance which is Enlightenment.

Yet initial Enlightenment brings further spiritual dangers of which the practitioner must be acutely aware. Chinese culture is intuitively attuned to possibilities of change or transformation in every situation. Concerning this state of After Completion, the oracle commentary warns: *It is just when perfect equilibrium has been reached that any movement may cause order to revert to disorder. . . . Hence the present hexagram indicates conditions in a time of climax which necessitates the utmost caution.* The primal harmony which can be discovered as the essence of all beings and their ways of life is not a static condition of perfection but a dynamic current in which one can easily lose balance. Equilibrium must be continuously sustained among ever-changing circumstances. Thus every detail of thought and action becomes intensely significant after the initial experience of illumination, for it is in the realm of detail that the awakened awareness must stay awake. Explains the oracle concerning this *new time*, or Enlightenment: *The transition from the old to the new time is already accomplished. . . . However, we must be careful to maintain the right attitude. Everything proceeds as if of its own accord, and this can too easily tempt us to relax and let things take their course without troubling over details.* Riding effortlessly on the flow of primal harmony does not exclude responsibility or concern. Enlightened beings observe a disciplined caring for every detail, an intense mindfulness. One such fully illumined person, Sarada Devi, wife of Ramakrishna, was watching someone sweep the porch. When the woman finished, she tossed the broom into a corner. Sarada admonished her: *Even the broom should be treated with care and respect.* Someone brought Sarada a fiber basket containing fruit. The person offered the fruit on the shrine and threw the basket on the trash heap. Sarada quietly went outside, retrieved the basket, carefully washed it, and put it on the shelf. Perhaps such attentiveness balances the bliss that arises spontaneously in the illumined consciousness. Such bliss can lead the practitioner into transcendental moods rather than sustaining the daily wakefulness in primal awareness which is Enlightenment.

The oracle continues to urge carefulness for those who have had an initial experience of Enlightenment or, in terms of this hexagram, who are existing in the condition of After Completion. *Water over fire: the image of the condition in After Completion. . . . When water in a kettle hangs over fire, two elements stand in relation and thus generate energy, the production of steam. The resulting tension demands caution. If the water boils over, the fire is extinguished and its energy is lost. If the heat is too great, the water evaporates into the air.* The mindfulness or equilibrium of Enlightenment must continuously maintain a balance which resembles this delicate interaction between water and fire. The primal harmony among beings and their ways of life must be rediscovered moment to moment through subtly changing conditions. We must not be lulled to sleep by a blissful glimpse of harmony.

The oracle continues: *In life there are junctures when all forces are in balance and work in harmony . . . only the sage recognizes the moments that bode danger and knows how to banish it by means of timely precautions.* The sage is the illumined teacher. Whether he or she is encountered in person or evoked through the oracles or sacraments of various traditions, we need guidance from the sage if we are to balance the powerful energies encountered in the universe or in the mind. The spiritual dimension of culture serves to open our access to such deep guidance by creating ritual situations in which primal harmony, the Divine Source or Tao, is revealed to us through languages and images we can understand.

The oracle has responded to our present request for guidance through the complex web of spiritual paths with the assurance that we are at a *turning point,* that there is the possibility of *return* to primal harmony in which the infinite diversity of beings and their ways can be experienced as a flow of symphonic music. However, the oracle warns us that after this mystical Return, when we exist in the condition called After Completion, the need for wakefulness or mindfulness increases. We are to move with Confucian caution and concern through the Taoist flow of natural, effortless harmony.

I performed the ritual cast of coins again, this time questioning the oracle about the essential nature of phenomena, which are collectively called the universe. Are not all forms of energy simply crystallizations of Ultimate Consciousness? Although it appears substantial and should be accepted as real on the level of ordinary experience, is not the world fundamentally dreamlike in nature?

The oracle, responding as an archetypal Chinese sage, dismissed the metaphysical question and recommended commitment to the universe, whatever its essential nature may be. The toss of coins indicated Hexagram 18: Work on What Has Been Spoiled. The mood is Confucian concern for the welfare of human beings as they struggle in the midst of ignorance and decay. Reads the commentary: *The Chinese character Ku represents a bowl in whose contents worms are breeding. This means decay. It has come about because the gentle indifference of the lower trigram has come together with the rigid inertia of the upper, and the result is stagnation.* Decay is here used as a symbol for the suffering experienced in the human world, this bowl which has not been properly cleaned and cared for. The *spoiling* of the human realm springs from a disharmony between two dimensions of our being, represented by the lower and upper trigrams in the configuration of the present hexagram. These two dimensions are the active and the contemplative, or in traditional Chinese imagery, earth and heaven. Enlightenment is the healing of this disharmony or dichotomy, which allows heavenly contemplation to transcend its own subtle inertia and transforms earthly indifference or stagnation into compassionate activity for the welfare of all. Heaven and earth are seen by the Enlightened person to interact perfectly as radiant clarity and compassionate concern. The oracle is requiring from us a commitment: *The conditions embody a demand for removal of the cause, hence the meaning of the hexagram is not simply "what has been spoiled" but "work on what has been spoiled."*

In every culture, spiritual withdrawal from the world is based to some degree on authentic insight into the dreamlike or insubstantial nature of the manifest universe. However, such withdrawal intensifies the contemplative inertia and the practical indifference which this hexagram recognizes as the cause of human suffering. Withdrawal from the world into contemplation represents a failure to perceive the mystical union of Shiva and Shakti, Yang and Yin, Heaven and Earth—a failure to follow the process of Enlightenment far enough. Further deepening of Enlightenment will make a significant difference in the quality of daily human life. As the oracle states: *Work on what has been spoiled has supreme success. What has been spoiled through man's fault can be made good again through man's work.* The power of transcendent contemplation which has correctly perceived the dreamlike nature of the universe should now be put to work to transform the human dream.

Ultimate Consciousness, which the illumined being realizes to be the essential nature of our universe, cannot be *spoiled*. This knowledge of intrinsic purity can become an intense force for practical service in the realm that human beings have *spoiled* through selfish indifference. Such service would be based on contemplative or heavenly understanding, not on the earthly ambition to dominate or control. The Enlightened person works for the transformation of human suffering without being overwhelmed by its vastness, because the illusory, or dreamlike, nature of this suffering is clearly understood. The mother who wakes her crying child from a nightmare understands that it is merely a dream, but this does not dim her sense of urgency and commitment. Knowing that her child is suffering merely in dream gives the mother quiet confidence as she sets about to awaken it.

The oracle suggests that suffering springs from human disharmony and is not the intrinsic nature of Consciousness.

Through the process of Enlightenment, which includes compassionate action on all levels, this situation of suffering or *corruption* can be transformed. Reads the commentary: *It is not immutable fate . . . that has caused the state of corruption but, rather, the abuse of human freedom. Work toward improving conditions promises well.* With the right commitment the spiritual practitioner can significantly reduce the amount of suffering in the universe. We should use all approaches, from social or political action based on genuine compassion to the teaching of contemplative traditions which heal the apparent dichotomy between heaven and earth.

What is called for is total dedication of our energy to the welfare of humanity regarded as one family. This is not simply a high ideal but an actual practice. As the oracle explains: *We must not recoil from work and danger . . . but must take hold energetically.* In this same spirit of energy and commitment, Vivekananda used to remark: *I worship and serve God in the form of the poor, the sick, the ignorant, and the oppressed.* This is not armchair metaphysical work, though it must have a strong metaphysical and contemplative basis. The work is dangerous, not only physically but also spiritually, for involvement with the world's problems can subtly disorient our own spiritual balance, and without heavenly balance we can only compound earthly suffering. As the oracle suggests: *Success depends on proper deliberation.* Confucian responsibility, mature spiritual commitment to the welfare of the planet is grounded in deliberation and contemplation. We cannot transform the confusion of the world without having overcome this confusion through Enlightenment, which not only allows us to perceive the root causes of human disharmony but also to tap the inexhaustible power of primal harmony. From this foundation of Enlightenment, our commitment and energy can be permanently sustained without any selfish motivation. Continues the oracle: *We must first know the causes of corruption before we can do away with them.* There are real causes for suffering, but only contemplative insight can penetrate them and envision the *new way,* which removes the roots of suffering rather than simply relieving its symptoms. Advises the oracle: We *must see to it that the new way is safely entered upon, so that a relapse may be avoided. . . . Decisiveness and energy must take the place of the inertia and indifference that have led to decay.* The need for wakeful energy intensifies as contemplation is being linked with compassionate action, or else heaven and earth will again appear to move away from each other.

The oracle presents this image: *The wind blows low on the mountain. Thus the superior person stirs up the people and strengthens their spirit.* We are being counseled to take broad action in the social context, not simply to concentrate on spiritual growth among a few advanced contemplatives. Proclaims the oracle: *The superior person must regenerate society.* This *superior person* is simply the awakening person, in no way innately superior to other human beings, who stimulates the conscience and active concern of the entire human family to *work on what has been spoiled* while remaining grounded in the contemplation of primal harmony. The oracle continues: *The superior person must first remove stagnation by stirring up public opinion, as the wind stirs everything, and must ever strengthen . . . the character of the people, as the mountain gives tranquillity and nourishment to all that grows in its vicinity.* The ideal here is that of intensely wakeful concern in the midst of serenity. We must express both the dynamic *wind* of compassionate action and the tranquil, fertile *mountainside* of contemplation. The oracle is exhorting us to nourish people on all levels of their hunger. Full commitment to the life of the human family is the Chinese Way.

The third question I posed to the oracle was how to embrace all phenomena as expressions of Divine Nature, or in Chinese terms, as the Tao. How can we awaken into Enlightenment? The response was Hexagram 45: Gathering Together. Explains the commentary: *This hexagram is related in form and meaning to Holding Together. In the latter, water is over the earth; here a lake is over the earth. But since the lake is a place where water collects, the idea of gathering together is even more strongly expressed here than in the other hexagram.* This is the complete gathering together of all phenomena, the integrating experience or understanding that we have termed Enlightenment. Heavenly and earthly dimensions are no longer held apart. For the Enlightened sage, there is total involvement with all forms of life as Divine Life, or Tao. The Way of Tao, like the Tantric Way, involves *gathering together* as a single essence all thoughts and perceptions, all heavenly and earthly forms. Nothing is excluded.

The process of Enlightenment described by this hexagram, the *gathering together* of all phenomena, is not a simple project one can undertake in isolation. The oracle counsels: *It furthers one to see the great person.* This way is difficult and even dangerous, requiring the guidance of the sage, or guru. We must also make use of authentic forms of liturgy from sacred tradition. In the language of the oracle, offerings are to be made in the temple: *Gathering together. Success. The king approaches his temple. . . . To bring great offerings creates good fortune.*

This regenerative gathering together or unification of all worlds and beings in the sacred dimension of the temple under the guidance of the sage, or *great person*, is expressed by the oracle through the metaphor of gathering people together: *The gathering together of people in a large community is either a natural occurrence, as in the case of the family, or an artificial one, as in the case of the state. The perpetuation of this gathering in groups is achieved through the sacrifice to the Ancestors, at which the whole clan is gathered together.* The unifying, or integrating, process of Enlightenment does not resemble the artificial organization of people into the state but resembles the natural form of Gathering Together expressed by the family. All beings and phenomena are experienced by the Enlightened sage as one clan, one intrinsic nature or Tao, flowing as a single stream.

The liturgy of Gathering Together is characterized by the oracle as sacrificing to the Ancestors. Central to the process of Enlightenment in many traditions is contemplative unification of our individual being with the being of various protecting and guiding Deities, our metaphysical Ancestors. In the context of Chinese spiritual culture, human Ancestors function as Deities. Through the sacrificial offering of our separate being to the Ancestors, the guiding and protecting power of the heavenly family becomes deeply integrated and expressed in the life of the earthly family. This is the process of integration, Gathering Together, or Enlightenment. As the commentary explains: *Through the collective piety of the living members of the family, the Ancestors become so integrated in the spiritual life of the family that it cannot be dispersed or dissolved.* Through intense and disciplined invocation of the Deities, or Ancestors, they become living manifestations. Advanced practitioners converse face to face with various Deities, but the integration of Gathering Together goes further than transcendental visions. All earthly as well as heavenly forms are now seen as members of the same Family of Consciousness gathered around the *great person*, or Enlightened sage.

The oracle explains this focus on the living sage: *Where people are to be gathered together, religious forces are needed. But there must also be a human leader to serve as the center of the group. In order to be able to bring others together, this leader must first of all be collected within himself.* In order to embrace all as the Tao, or True Way, we must follow the guidance of Enlightened human beings who have *gathered together*, or integrated, every living being, every Ancestor, every phenomenon, every Deity into a single flow. They experience only the Tao, free from any sense of separation or fragmentation. While clinging to our own separateness, we cannot awaken to the process of Gathering Together, or Enlightenment. Subtle and intense obstacles or distortions will arise. As the oracle warns, sacred forces are needed. The various protecting and guiding forces of Spirit are linked with certain elements in our own psyche and the collective psyche that need to be propitiated in order safely to dissolve the barriers between beings and the separation between Heaven and Earth. These protecting and guiding forces are ideally to be focused through the *great person,* or sage, who can speak to us intelligently and intimately in the role of spiritual friend and guide.

The oracle warns us to cultivate alertness as we remain afloat in contemplation on the lake of all phenomena. *Over the earth, the lake: the image of Gathering Together. Thus the superior person renews his weapons in order to meet the unforeseen.* Only the awakened person knows what dangers, what subtle reactions and relapses may occur in the revolutionary process of Gathering Together, and how to prepare for them. Discriminations between pure and impure, good and evil, sacred and profane, are important forms of psychological protection. If we abandon these discriminations in the embrace of all as the Tao, we are dropping our ordinary protection. We must develop instead what the oracle calls *weapons:* devotion to Deities, or Ancestors, and clear insight into the Intrinsic nature we share with them as the Tao.

The oracle gives this illustration of possible danger: *If the water in the lake gathers until it rises above the earth, there is danger of a break-through. Precautions must be taken to prevent this.* Once while Ramakrishna was engaged in his perennial experimentation with various forms of spiritual practice, dark blood suddenly gushed from his nose and mouth. There happened to be an advanced yogi living in the temple garden at that time, who examined him and reported that had the rush of blood continued directly to the brain, Ramakrishna would have been killed instantly. All the volcanic energy of the universe exists in seed form within the human body and mind. There is danger of what the oracle calls a *break-through* of this energy. Insanity or even death can result if we play haphazardly at Gathering Together. As the oracle continues: *In the time of Gathering Together, we should make no arbitrary choice of the way. There are secret forces at work, leading together those who belong together. We must yield to this attraction; then we make no mistakes. Where inner relationships exist, no great preparations and formalities are necessary. People understand one another forthwith, just as the Divinity graciously accepts a small offering if it comes from the heart.* If we allow ourselves to be drawn intuitively to a spiritual guide and spiritual family with whom we feel an immediate natural relationship, our growth will occur safely. Strict ritual requirements then gradually evaporate. Sincerity becomes the only criterion. As the oracle suggests: *Letting oneself be drawn brings good fortune and remains blameless. If one is sincere, it furthers one to bring even a small offering.* Whatever our conception of the Deities, or Ancestors, if we can *let ourselves be drawn* into relationship with these forces of Spirit—the relationship of sincerity and purity of purpose—then our spiritual family will appear in various unexpected forms to receive and embrace us.

The spontaneity of our attraction to the sage, or guru, is the measure of its authenticity. Explains the commentary: *When people spontaneously gather around a person it is only good.* When spiritual attraction is inwardly quiet and authentic, not based on the charismatic powers or reputation of the guru or on the use of suggestion by his or her disciples, then the discipleship is fruitful. Concerning attraction to a teacher that is based on superficial motives, the oracle warns: *There is also the possibility that many may gather around him not because of a feeling of confidence but merely because of his influential position. This is certainly to be regretted.* Discipleship can become neurotic when it lacks purity of motivation or spontaneity of attraction, when either teacher or disciple is grasping the other.

Thus, after assuring us that Enlightenment or *gathering together* all phenomena as the Tao, is accessible through the sage, the oracle has once again evoked the mood of caution. The authentic sage is not only difficult to find but, once encountered, must be carefully appreciated as a person of love and wisdom rather than as a person of charismatic power.

I then sought guidance from the oracle concerning the correct attitude toward formal contemplative practice. The Taoist tendency to be suspicious of formal structure and strict control in spiritual life was manifest in the oracle's reply, Hexagram 47: Exhaustion or Oppression. *The lake is above, water below; the lake is empty, dried up. The upper trigram belongs to the principle of darkness, the lower to the principle of light. Thus everywhere superior persons are oppressed and held in restraint by inferior persons.* Held in restraint by formal spiritual disciplines or by dogmatic teachers, the practitioner can become dry. Strict ritual behavior and prescribed techniques of contemplation can become means of oppressing oneself and others, drying up the natural flow of our spiritual energy, restricting our intrinsic spiritual freedom.

Yet within the potential oppressiveness of spiritual discipline lies the seed of release. As the oracle hints: *Times of adversity are the reverse of times of success, but they can lead to success if they befall the right person.* Richly imbued with Taoist attitudes, the Zen Ox-herding pictures suggest that when we first begin to seek the Ox, or Tao, through spiritual discipline and concentration we are subject to the most intense illusion, for we imagine the Ox to be separate from our own True Nature. We undergo rigorous spiritual practices, or *times of adversity,* in order to find what has never been lost and therefore can never be found. The present hexagram, Exhaustion or Oppression, reflects this phase of adversity, austerity, or quest, which gradually disappears into the condition of no special seeking which is the Tao, or True Way.

The oracle counsels us to remain cheerful during our phase of formal practice: *When a strong person meets with adversity, he remains cheerful despite all danger . . . and this cheerfulness is the source of later successes. . . . He who lets his spirit be broken by exhaustion certainly has no success.* The person who is robbed of energy and freedom by the seriousness of spiritual discipline, which the oracle terms *exhaustion,* may never emerge from the phase of austerity, or illusory quest. But the person eventually succeeds who remains cheerful, appreciating the humor of seeking for our own primal awareness. As the oracle suggests: *If adversity only bends a person, it creates in him a power to react that is bound in time to manifest itself.* Many Enlightenment experiences reflect a spontaneous reaction against the intensely formal structure of sitting in meditation, which does indeed bend us, as a bow bends, giving us the power to transcend formal practice as the arrow suddenly springs from the bow. The very strictures that spiritual disciplines impose give us strength eventually to transcend those disciplines. Then we stand totally free and natural in the Tao.

My ritual toss of coins elicited a particularly strong warning concerning the oppressive nature of formal religious practices. The oracle states: *A man permits himself to be oppressed by stone, and leans on thorns and thistles. He enters his house and does not see his wife. Misfortune.* The stone, thorns, and thistles represent the rigors, or austerities, we impose on ourselves, falsely imagining that they will somehow lead us to Enlightenment. The person who *does not see his wife* represents the spiritual practitioner who lives in the world yet ignores his responsibility to the entire human family, wishing to transcend earth in favor of heaven, following the false assumption that earth is separate from heaven.

Chinese tradition has created apocryphal tales about meetings between Confucius and the Taoist master Lao-tzu. These tales reflect tensions between Confucian and Taoist approaches to the Tao, or True Way, although Chinese spiritual culture as a whole represents a blending of both these spiritual moods. Here is one such traditional story that illustrates the Taoist critique of systematic discipline which we have encountered in the response of the oracle. *Confucius unrolled a dozen treatises and began to expound them. Lao-tzu interrupted him and said, "This is going to take too long. Tell me the gist of the matter." "The gist of the matter," said Confucius, "is goodness and duty." "Would you tell me," said Lao-tzu, "are these qualities natural to man?" "Indeed, these are," said Confucius. Lao-tzu said, "If you indeed want the men of the world not to lose the qualities that are natural to them, if you don't want them to lose what they already have, you had best study how it is that heaven and earth maintain their eternal course. . . . What you are doing is to disjoint men's natures. Never help any man to perfect the unalloyed that is within him."* Formal spiritual practice is disjointing because it creates an imaginary process of perfecting our nature, which is already a perfect expression of the Tao. There is a close parallel between this Taoist attitude and Indian Tantric literature. Sings the ancient Bengali sage Saraha in one of his songs about the spontaneously born Enlightenment of the Sahajayana, or Natural Way: *Mantras and tantras, meditation and concentration, they are all a cause of self-deception. Do not defile by contemplation thought that is pure in its own nature, but abide in the bliss of yourself and cease these torments.* Enlightenment is a delicate natural balance which we need not disturb in any way. Human suffering or disharmony is simply the disturbance of that innate sense of balance which is the *unalloyed, pure in its own nature.*

The hexagram of Exhaustion or Oppression was transformed in my particular toss of the coins into Hexagram 29, the Abysmal, further evoking the danger of formal spiritual practice, although suggesting as well a way through this phase. Interpreting the configuration of the hexagram, the commentary reads: . . . *a yang line has plunged in between two yin lines and is closed in by them like water in a ravine.* By various exercises of concentration, we confine our energy, forcing it to accelerate dangerously, like water in a ravine, rather than simply allowing primal awareness to express itself harmoniously as the Tao. In this hexagram, the water is a symbol for our intrinsic nature, or primal awareness, which takes every shape as it flows. The essence of our being, the *unalloyed*, is awareness, self-purifying and self-clarifying because, like water, it is naturally pure and transparent.

The flow of primal awareness has now been focused into the narrow ravine of formal spiritual practice. Explains the commentary: *The name of the hexagram, because the trigram is doubled, has the additional meaning "repetition of danger."* There is constant psychological danger in this narrowest and most precipitous of all ravines. It is more dangerous to our innate sense of balance to be spiritual seekers than to have no pretensions to spirituality, although we must pass through this phase of formal discipline on the way to Enlightenment.

Water in a ravine

Reads the commentary: *A ravine is used to symbolize danger . . . a situation in which a person is in the same pass as the water in a ravine, and, like the water, he can escape if he behaves correctly.* The ravine of spiritual discipline increases the force and the speed of the water, and so, if we respond by plunging forward with abandon, we can transcend the danger. Explains the commentary: *Water sets the example for the right conduct under such circumstances. It flows on and on, and merely fills up all the places through which it flows; it does not shrink from any dangerous spot nor from any plunge, and nothing can make it lose its own essential nature. It remains true to itself under all conditions.* Plunging forward courageously leads the practitioner into further dimensions of Enlightenment.

To remain identified with any of the earlier phases of spiritual development is to be locked into the dangerous illusions we are warned of by this hexagram. What the advanced spiritual practitioner eventually discovers, not intellectually but with the total impact of direct experience, is that, in the language of the oracle, our *essential nature remains true to itself under all conditions.* What transforms the practitioner into the sage is the realization that Enlightenment is perfect all along the way. Nothing can cause primal awareness to lose its essential nature, whether we are dreaming or waking, praying to a certain Deity, sacrificing to a particular Ancestor, or contemplating the Tao.

The counsel of the oracle concerning spiritual practice is contained in the image of flow. While the Tao, or primal awareness, is never structured, the rite of passage, the plunge through the ravine of formal discipline, is unavoidable. But the essential nature of the flow is ever pure and ever the same. Both beginner and sage share the same essential nature as Tao, or primal flow. As the oracle suggests: *Water reaches its goal by flowing continuously. It fills up every depression before it flows on. The superior person follows its example.* This is the natural way. Every depression is filled, no dimension of life is excluded or left unfulfilled. Enlightenment is revealed as the effortlessly flowing nature of all Consciousness, rather than falsely imagined to be an isolated occurrence for one being or another at one time or another.

(5) The final question I posed the oracle concerned the nature of the philosophical mind and its pursuit of coherent, balanced understanding. Remarkably, considering that there are sixty-four possible hexagrams, the coin ritual again yielded Hexagram 29, the Abysmal, indicating the danger of formal structure in intellectual as well as spiritual pursuit. But in the present response of the oracle, the Taoist warning against structure was transformed into the Confucian affirmation of design, since the Abysmal was changed, according to this toss of the coins, into the hexagram of the Well, which symbolizes the centering of society.

The quest for philosophical understanding is subject to the same danger as formal spiritual practice, because both involve focusing and concentrating, structuring and organizing awareness. The secret is to allow the water of awareness to flow. In philosophical pursuit we must not force the patterns perceived by the intellect to become fixed, or rigid. The intellect must flow through these patterns, and the patterns themselves must melt and flow in continuous evolution.

The direction in which the philosophically investigative mind moves, once these dangers of the Abysmal are transcended, was indicated by the oracle through Hexagram 48, the Well. The image presented is one of harmonious function. The living water of awareness no longer plunges dangerously through the ravine but serves as nourishment for society. States the commentary: *The well from which water is drawn conveys the ideal of inexhaustible dispensing of nourishment.* Authentic philosophical investigation is not an abstract game but a reliable source of life-giving nourishment. Mature philosophical thinking, which is the water in this archetypal Well, is the same water that plunges through the ravine, the water of our essential nature, which has now been channeled to serve basic human needs. As well as flowing wildly through the mountains, the water of primal awareness springs up serenely in the daily life of humanity, safeguarding the balance of the individual and the society. The oracle remarks: *The town may be changed, but the well cannot be changed. It neither decreases nor increases. They come and go and draw from the well.*

The commentary further explains: *In ancient China the capital cities were sometimes moved, partly for the sake of more favorable location, partly because of a change in dynasties.* This is the process of intellectual history in which different world views arise, take shape, and disappear in endless transformation, while the Well, the intellect, the medium of philosophical understanding, remains the same archetypal presence. The commentary continues: *The style of architecture changed in the course of centuries, but the shape of the well has remained the same from ancient times to this day. Thus the well is the symbol of that social structure which, evolved by mankind in meeting its most primitive needs, is independent of all political forms.* The life-giving water of the Well symbolizes pure intelligence, the energy of thinking or inquiring, which is independent of all particular philosophical, scientific, artistic, religious, and political forms. Countless individuals gather around the Well to draw nourishment for their diverse cultural moments, but the process of drawing water and the water itself remain the same. Explains the commentary: *Political structures change, as do nations, but the life of man with its needs remains eternally the same—this cannot be changed. Life is inexhaustible. It grows neither less nor more; it exists for one and for all. The generations come and go, and all enjoy life in its inexhaustible abundance.* This is the Chinese sense of inexhaustible Life, which, although in continuous transformation, always abides as the Tao, or True Way. Through the medium of the Well, we tap this Life as intellect or intelligence, creating designs for social and personal existence. This use of the intellect is not confined to scientists or scholars but belongs to all people who gather around the Well to meet the basic need for understanding.

Still, drawing water from the Well is a process that has its own complications and dangers. This is suggested by the oracle: *If one gets down almost to the water and the rope does not go all the way or the jug breaks, it brings misfortune.* We must reach deep to draw the water of intelligence. As the commentary explains: *For a satisfactory political or social organization of mankind* (or for a satisfactory philosophical world view) *we must go down to the very foundations of life. Any merely superficial ordering of life that leaves its deepest needs unsatisfied is as ineffectual as if no attempt at order had ever been made. Carelessness —by which the jug is broken—is also disastrous.* Superficiality is thinking that is one-sided rather than panoramic; carelessness is thinking that lacks the discipline of clarity. To inquire philosophically, we must develop the balance of the tightrope walker, who is risking his or her own life. Philosophical investigation cannot be mere casual speculation. Standards of coherence must be met, yet these standards are not mechanically binding rules of logic by which any particular proposition can be identified as valid or invalid. Philosophy is not a technical academic enterprise but intuitive thinking that profoundly embodies principles of coherence, slaking our thirst with water from the Well.

The oracle commentary explains the image of the short rope and the broken jug: *Every human being can draw in the course of his education from the inexhaustible well-spring of the divine in man's nature. But here likewise two dangers threaten: a person may fail in his education to penetrate to the real roots of humanity and remain fixed in convention . . . or he may suddenly collapse and neglect his self-development.* Any person can draw from the Well, intellectually trained or not, who thinks in depth, at the *real roots of humanity*, and who sustains deep commitment to *self-development* or the process of Enlightenment. The dimension of intellect, as the oracle reveals, intersects the dimension of Spirit, *the divine in man's nature.*

During an earlier conversation with the oracle, I inquired about the spiritual implications of philosophical investigation. The response was Hexagram 50, the Cauldron, sister hexagram to the Well. While water from the Well nourishes

cauldron
vs
Well

our practical and intellectual being, the Cauldron holds nourishment for our Spirit. The oracle commentary explains: *The
Cauldron, cast of bronze, was the vessel that held the cooked offerings
in the temple of the ancestors.* The Well provides the indispensable nourishment of mental alertness and creativity, the
clear water necessary for all daily purposes. But the nourishment held by the Cauldron is more potent, rare, and intense. Reads the commentary: *The well relates to the social
foundation of our life* (or to our intellectual resources), *and this
foundation is likened to the water that serves to nourish growing
wood. The present hexagram, the Cauldron, refers to the cultural
super-structures of society* (or to our spiritual resources). *Here
it is the wood that serves as nourishment for the flame, the spirit.*
The water of the Well, or intelligence, nourishes the grove
of social and philosophical structures, whose wood eventually serves to feed the flame of Spirit in the sacrificial offering.

The commentary continues: *All that is visible must grow
beyond itself, extend into the realm of the invisible. Thereby it
receives its true consecration and clarity and takes firm root in the
cosmic order. Here we see civilization as it reaches its culmination
in religion. The Cauldron serves in offering sacrifice to God. The
highest earthly values must be sacrificed to the divine. But the truly
divine does not manifest itself apart from man.* Divine Nature
does not manifest to us apart from human nature but is
expressed fully as our primal awareness, which illumined
sages experience as the Tao. Thus the Enlightened sage *is*
the Cauldron, the vessel in which earth and heaven blend
in sacred alchemy. Explains the commentary: *The supreme
revelation of God appears in prophets and holy persons. To venerate
them is true veneration of God. The will of God, as revealed through
them, should be accepted in humility; this brings inner enlightenment and true understanding of the world, and this leads to
great good fortune and success.* To venerate the awakened sage
is not actually to focus on a particular human being but to
celebrate the Tao, or primal awareness, expressed through
all beings.

As the oracle suggests, the wood nourished by the water of intelligence is eventually burned to heat the alchemical Cauldron. All social, artistic, scientific, and philosophical enterprises provide fuel for the sacrificial fire of Spirit. Without this fuel there would be no flame, no transformation, no Enlightenment. This is the intimate connection between humanity's intellectual and artistic creativity and its spiritual illumination. The structures of mind and culture are ignited and consumed by spiritual vision. All earthly and heavenly being is thereby blended or integrated in the Cauldron of primal awareness.

CHAPTER TEN

DESIGNING AN EXPERIMENT IN CONTEMPLATION

Toward the Turiya of Advaita Vedanta

The various ways to Enlightenment we have explored can all be described as contemplative, but we have not discussed in depth the actual practice of prayer and meditation that constitutes contemplative life. Therefore we offer here a spiritual experiment that can be undertaken by anyone who wishes to glimpse from within the nature of contemplative practice. This experiment is designed to be general enough to accommodate all sacred traditions with their moods of devotion and wisdom, or to be used apart from any religious imagery.

We speak of this as an *experiment* in order to distinguish these universal suggestions for prayer and meditation from spiritual instructions given directly by a teacher immersed in one particular tradition. Every seeker should receive traditional initiation and personal guidance from at least one authentic spiritual guide. Then one no longer simply *experiments* with contemplation but *lives* contemplative practice. But the present experiment can provide a useful global perspective not only for those who have never received traditional spiritual instruction but also for those involved primarily in one particular sacred tradition.

As we explore various methods for controlling, heightening, or clarifying awareness, we should remember the profound teaching of Enlightened persons from various cultures: harmonious and balanced living is not only the preparation for contemplation but also the practice of contemplation and its ultimate goal. The contemplative mood is the essence of our consciousness, not a condition to be imposed on it. Furthermore, the intrinsic nature of planetary life, wherever it occurs in the universe, and even the nature of Being itself, are spontaneously contemplative.

Understanding that contemplation is primarily to live consciously and only secondarily involves formal practice, we can then choose maturely a mode of contemplative life, a particular discipline of prayer or meditation. This is comparable to dance. If we can regard bodily movement as already dance, then when we enter some particular form of dance training, our appreciation of natural grace and spontaneity is deepened, not lost in the rigor or theory of the training. Similarly, as we transform our lives into formal liturgical, contemplative dance, we should retain complete freedom of movement. This freedom is the mystical sense that understands perfect prayer or meditation as the core of our being, spontaneously springing from the core of Being itself. The beautiful structure of our spiritual practice should grow directly from the structureless ground of primal awareness. We should enjoy simultaneously the vision of the formal structure and its formless Source. Many seekers who undertake spiritual life through religious commitment or esoteric study become too concerned with the aspect of structure. The opposite distortion is the refusal to recognize the value of structured practice. The person who has a narrowly structured or exclusive sense of spiritual practice can at least begin to develop, like a seed, planted in a small pot, which can later be transplanted in an open field. The person without a spiritual practice, however, is like a seed without soil: it can germinate but cannot send down roots.

As we explore various forms of contemplation, we should

also remember that personal moral development provides the only reliable foundation for such experiments. Compassion and clarity are the fruits of moral discipline, which is not mechanical application of a system that defines certain acts and impulses as good or evil but is, rather, the continuous effort to express truthfulness and loving concern through all behavior and thinking. Without the balance created by this moral discipline, we could distort contemplative practice and the intoxicating experiences it can produce. Honesty with ourselves and responsiveness to others provides a ground for the potentially dangerous electricity of spiritual life.

Prayer or meditation is a liturgical act, but it depends on our own particular temperament how elaborate or outwardly visible this liturgy becomes. Whatever way we choose, we should be aware that the magic circle, or mandala, of contemplative practice must be drawn with reverence and care. The evocation of the prayerful or meditative mood may be simple but never careless or haphazard. Traditional texts describe every detail concerning the ritual of contemplation, including the construction of the shrine or the visualization of body and mind as the shrine. But the secular attitude of contemporary society may have its value as a balance to excessive ritualism. We need not retreat to a completely traditional atmosphere, where every detail of life is formal or liturgical. Yet we must remain receptive to the formal disciplines of contemplation, which may include chanting certain prayers or mantras, wearing special clothes, eating particular diets, learning new languages, and engaging in various esoteric forms of physical and mental training. Our original moral commitment to truthfulness and compassion will keep these practices from becoming merely theatrical.

As an example of contemplative liturgy we can consider the breath-watching meditation of Theravada Buddhism. Theravada tradition regards this practice not only as an easy access for beginners to the contemplative mood but also as a practice powerful enough to carry us through all the stages of evolution to full Enlightenment. The Buddha is said to

have practiced breath-watching as a mode of refreshment even after his Enlightenment. This is a universal practice which we can now attempt together, whatever our religious commitment or absence of commitment may be. The calming, concentrating, and deepening of our awareness through this spiritual practice can be considered a preparation for entering the four dimensions of contemplation which we will discuss later.

Watching the breath provides perhaps the most intimate, tangible access to primal awareness that is easily available to the spiritual practitioner. The breath can be immediately observed not only in a quiet mood but even when attention is distracted in various ways. Theravada tradition points out that breath is one of the few meditation objects that one can actually touch. The practitioner is not thinking about breath, in the sense of imagining or visualizing, but is touching it continuously. In traditional texts the formal practice of watching the breath is described in four successive stages.

1. The first stage is slow counting: the inbreath and outbreath are counted as one, the following inbreath and outbreath as two. This process continues to ten, and then begins again from one. Slow counting is carried on until various thoughts and perceptions, though continuing to arise, no longer cause us to lose count.

2. In the second stage, although breath is becoming calmer, the counting is faster and thus more involving. The inbreath is one, the outbreath two, the following inbreath three, the following outbreath four, continuing until ten and beginning again from one. We are now counting twice as fast, and thus begin to join the breaths together, rather than regarding each inbreath and outbreath as a separate entity. This faster counting is continued until the separate breaths begin to disappear into a continuous flow of breath awareness.

3. In the third stage, counting ceases. Since the breath is experienced to be continuous, there is nothing to count. At this point there occurs what tradition terms the *contact* sign. This sign appears, as the texts carefully explain, on the upper

lip if we are flat-nosed, or inside the tip of the nose if we are long-nosed. This is where the inbreath and the outbreath strike. This point becomes a mandala, a field in which awareness is concentrated and which shimmers in our consciousness as an orb shimmers in our vision when we gaze at the sun and then look away. We now cease watching the breath as a cyclical flow. Our focus becomes simply this contact sign, this shimmering presence of awareness. Other thoughts and perceptions disappear or become peripheral. Traditional texts give the example of sawing wood. The saw touches only one point. That is where the concentration of the woodsman is placed, for that is where the power of the process is focused and where the transformation occurs.

4. The fourth stage involves leaving behind not only breath but the entire web of body and mind. The contact sign begins to transform. The texts explain that various visionary experiences can occur. The contact sign may appear as sparks or feel like cotton or mist. These experiences reflect subtle events in our nervous system as awareness becomes more and more concentrated. Then the meditator is instructed to move the contact sign, the mandala of awareness, to the space between the eyebrows. Here it ceases to be the contact sign, for there is nothing now to contact or to be contacted. The crystallization of consciousness which we call the body and mind, when focused in this way through the psychic center between the eyebrows, gradually melts into primal awareness.

This practice of breath-watching concentrates more and more finely on the body-mind, gradually refining our awareness until the body-mind is revealed as the radiance of Ultimate Consciousness. We could now visualize, emerging from this primal radiance and sharing its intrinsic nature, whatever images appeal to us from various sacred traditions. Or we could remain simply with the radiance of primal awareness itself. We should now briefly attempt these four levels of practice, bearing in mind that actual mastery of even the first level might require weeks of patient endeavor.

In Buddhist breath-watching there is no attempt consciously to shorten, slow down, or stop the breath. One attempts to attune simply and naturally to the continuousness, or oneness, of breath. Yet during the course of this practice we spontaneously experience what the tradition calls *subtle breathing*. The following illustration is offered by the ancient texts. Our ordinary breathing compares to subtle breathing as the breath of a person climbing a hill compares to the breath of this same person fully rested on top of the hill. What we think of as relaxed breathing is ragged and frantic compared with subtle breathing. Gazing from this hilltop of subtle breathing allows us to perceive the body-mind as the radiance of Ultimate Consciousness.

By practicing the contemplation of breath at any of its four stages, our awareness gradually becomes more calm and more intense. Upon this universal foundation, we can create further liturgies of prayer and meditation, using the basic components of mood, mantra, and visualization. We can each design our own unique experiment in contemplation.

We should begin by choosing a contemplative mood that is appropriate to our own temperament, a mode of intuition or feeling in which our spiritual practice will develop, as a symphony develops in a particular key. We can speak of four basic contemplative moods: energy, love, peace, and insight. We may wish eventually to blend the four, as a composer modulates through various keys, but we should select a central mood in which to begin our experiment. Each basic mood has its own characteristic conceptions of Reality, its particular attitudes toward contemplative practice and spiritual experience—structural similarities that underlie the infinite variety of spiritual moods in various cultures.

The mood of *energy* attunes us to all forms of creative action. Our body, mind, and spirit absorb the power streaming from the core of life. Every breath affirms life and communion with all lives. No doctrine of a personal God is necessary here. We simply contemplate the transcendental Sun of pure conscious energy at the Source of the universe, translating this contemplation into action by building and serving.

In the mood of *love*, various manifestations of the Supreme Person are evoked as the essential nature of Reality. We experience the ecstasy of communing, through our own personhood, with the ultimate personhood of the Divine. We contemplate Divine Love assuming holy forms to guide, nurture, and protect all beings. We engage with joyous intensity in various forms of worship and prayer, and cherish all persons as images of the Divine.

In the mood of *peace*, we move toward the ideal of utter cessation, or liberation, the plunge into transcendent Godhead. We contemplate the lake of pure Consciousness, still as a mirror, undisturbed by the winds of desire. Our only concern is that all human beings eventually experience the Absolute, in which persons and events completely disappear into their Source.

In the mood of *insight*, we regard all phenomena as sharing the same intrinsic nature. This single essence is simultaneously at rest as the transcendent Absolute and at play as the drama of existence. There is neither bondage nor liberation. We contemplate the identity of our own essential nature as primal awareness with the essential nature of all phenomena, earthly and heavenly. We delight in all forms while perceiving them as perfectly transparent configurations of Consciousness.

Having selected a central contemplative mood, to be developed and explored according to our own feeling and intuition, we can choose a mantra. The essence of mantra practice is repetition, which is not hypnotic but revealing. Co-ordinated with each cycle of our breathing, which has become more subtle through breath-watching practice, we should now mentally repeat over and over again one brief prayer, invocation, phrase, single word, or even simple sound which evokes the particular contemplative mood we have chosen. This mantra, which we experimentally select or which reveals itself to us, may not spring from the ambiance of any particular sacred tradition: whatever word or phrase we repeat as our mantra should simply have the power to evoke for us the mood of energy, love, peace, or insight.

Corresponding to the sound of the mantra, which, although not repeated aloud, rings through our entire awareness, is the light of our visualization. The selection of an image to visualize resembles the selection of a mantra. We may imagine as emerging from the radiance of primal awareness any human or divine figure, any earthly or heavenly vista or object that functions as a sacrament for us, focusing our particular contemplative mood. The inward sound of the mantra and the inner light of the visualization fuse and shimmer musically at the center of our conscious being. This center, which is the temple, or ground, of our contemplative practice, can be envisioned as a radiant Presence two fingers to the right of the breastbone.

The Sanskrit term for this visualized image is *ishtadeva*, the chosen ideal or guiding Divinity of our contemplation. Any traditional manifestation of the Divine can become our ishtadeva: Shiva, Allah, Christ, Krishna, Buddha, Yahweh, or one of the myriad forms of the Goddess, such as Kali, Tara, or Mary. Our ishtadeva could also be a living human being whom we love and respect as a guide or simply a spiritual quality such as peace or harmony, truth or compassion. Even if our particular ishtadeva is impossible to represent as an image, its Presence or Reality is attuned to by visualizing associated symbolic forms such as certain holy texts, teachers, and places of pilgrimage or natural beauty. Whether our ishtadeva is a sparkling Void, a Sacred Mountain, or a Holy Child, the essence of the contemplative process remains the same.

The practice of contemplation begins with visualization as a conscious effort of imagination, but gradually develops into mystical vision of the ishtadeva. This is the realm of spiritual experience where one perceives or feels the powerful presence of the ishtadeva without any effort at imagination. Contem-

plation becomes revelation. We can discern four dimensions
of contemplation in which the ishtadeva reveals itself in four
different modes. To complete this experiment in contemplation, we should immerse our awareness successively in each
of these four revelatory modes, using our own particular
mood, mantra, and ishtadeva. Through this act of spiritual
imagination, we can glimpse for ourselves the nature of revelatory experience.

The first dimension is prayerful contemplation. The Form
or Presence of the ishtadeva, or chosen ideal, is invoked by
the mantra and appears as vibrantly alive, composed from
the radiance of Consciousness. We are not projecting the
ishtadeva. The primal radiance which assumes the form of
the ishtadeva is actually projecting us and all the phenomena
that we call the universe. The ishtadeva that we have chosen
represents the archetype, or door of power, through which
we originally emerged from primal radiance and through
which we now seek to return or to come home. In this first
dimension of contemplation, the mystical kinship between
the practitioner and the ishtadeva, or guiding Divinity, expresses itself initially as reverence or awe and then, gradually, as friendship or nearness. Prayer and worship of the
Divine mellows into conversation or communion with the
Divine. This intimacy occurs whether or not the ishtadeva is
a personal being. The practitioner now receives inner guidance from the ishtadeva through words, images, or simply
its powerful Presence.

Full spiritual illumination can dawn for the practitioner
within this first dimension—prayerful contemplation—but
there is a second dimension, which intersects the first. In the
second dimension of contemplation, prayerfulness disappears into silent meditation as our sense of intimacy or communion with the ishtadeva deepens even further. The
contemplative and his or her chosen ideal blend with each
other and eventually merge completely. Gradually we realize
that the Divine Form or Presence is our own archetype, an
image of our own essential nature. But the ishtadeva does

not disappear into us; we as individuals disappear into the ishtadeva, which now remains alone. Yet there is no loss of our individual being as we blend into the object of our contemplation, for it has been our own archetype from the beginning, the source of this fragmentary reflection we call our individual personality. We remain now as a transcendental center of consciousness expressed through the Form or the formless Presence of the ishtadeva. We are now experiencing the life of the ishtadeva from within. We are consciously meeting and becoming ourselves in our archetypal and eternal nature.

While in the second dimension of contemplation our apparent self is consumed by the gemlike flame of its Divine Archetype, in the third dimension that Archetype itself dissolves into its own essence, or ground. At the heart of the ishtadeva is the primal radiance from which it has emerged, to which it returns, and into which it now disappears. Once again, there is nothing lost in this dissolution. The delight and value of all life-forms, earthly or transcendental, emanate from their essential nature as formless radiance. There is now perfect release into the radiance of formless Consciousness. There is no ishtadeva, no meditator, and no meditation, nor is there any awareness of an absence of these. There is only radiance. This third dimension of contemplation cannot involve any focus. We cannot pay attention to primal radiance, because there is nothing separate to pay attention to and no one to pay attention. And yet this radiance cannot be ignored, because it is pure attention.

This third dimension of contemplation should not be imagined as simply blank or empty. The world of mind and senses may sweep across the sky of pure Consciousness like clouds on a bright, windy day. Or the conscious sky may remain perfectly clear, yet radiantly aware. There need be no struggle to scatter the clouds of thought or sensation as if they could interrupt contemplation, for nothing can interruupt the primal radiance into which we and our ishtadeva have now disappeared. There is no need for meditation at all. Even if we tried, we could not ignore primal radiance, which is perfectly expressed by whatever thoughts occur, just as it is expressed by the absence of thought. This third dimension resembles the fulfillment that arises for the listener after the last chord of a symphony, when silence itself is experienced as pure music. The symphony of forms and archetypes has been moving and involving, but is now regarded as existing simply to deepen and accentuate the silence of primal radiance, which is gradually realized to be complete in itself, with or without forms or sounds. There is no sense in this third dimension of contemplation that forms or sounds ever really occur. They are at most transparent dreams.

Entering the fourth dimension of contemplation involves another unexpected transition. More subtle even than the move from archetypal form to formless radiance is the reappearance of our ishtadeva, manifesting as all human beings, all life-forms, all planets and galaxies throughout space and time, as well as all Divine Forms and their heavenly realms beyond physical space and time. We are still expressed through our particular Archetype and are so eternally, but this no longer involves any process of exclusion: all Archetypes interpenetrate perfectly. None of the other three dimensions of contemplation is obliterated in the fourth. The perfect Silence of the third dimension remains as the obverse of the universal music of the ishtadeva, which, in the fourth dimension, resonates as one Life on all planes. The first two dimensions are equally accessible: we can prayerfully converse or commune with the ishtadeva and we can disappear into the ishtadeva. The four dimensions interpenetrate without obstruction or exclusion.

In the first dimension of contemplation, we worship or contemplate a Divine Form or Presence. In the second dimension, the limited individual disappears and lives on as the Divine Form or Presence itself. In the third dimension, the Divine Form or Presence disappears into primal radiance. In the fourth dimension, this primal radiance in turn reveals itself as all patterns of Being, which reappear in an eternal stream, flowing from the core of the particular ishtadeva or Archetype that we are.

In the fourth dimension, nothing is excluded from our contemplation. Primal radiance and the infinite expressions of Life are fused. Our ishtadeva is everywhere. The holy sacraments of all cultures have become our sacraments, the ways of all beings have become our ways. Every content of consciousness proclaims the fusion of forms and the formless radiance that is their essence. At this moment, with open eyes, each of us is directly perceiving this fusion of all phenomena as primal radiance. It is not simply a contemplative notion. Even our physical senses, functioning in an ordinary manner, record this fusion. All is fusion. The four dimensions are one.

These four dimensions of contemplation echo the analysis of consciousness developed by the Advaita Vedanta school some fifteen hundred years ago on the Indian subcontinent. These ancient thinkers, who were primarily practitioners of contemplation, also speak of a fourfold configuration: three basic states of consciousness—waking, dream, dreamless sleep— and Turiya, which is not a particular state of consciousness but simply primal awareness itself.

The waking state presents to us a world of separate beings and is comparable to the first dimension of contemplation, in which there is separation between the worshiper and the object of worship or ishtadeva. In the dream state, beings tend to merge into each other, because the entire dream world is composed of our own consciousness, no matter how complicated or objective it appears. Thus the dream state is comparable to the second dimension of contemplation, in which the meditator merges into the object of meditation, realizing the ishtadeva to be the essence of his or her own consciousness. The state of dreamless sleep is comparable to the third dimension of contemplation, in which all forms disappear into formless radiance. And Turiya, which is the Sanskrit term meaning *fourth*, corresponds to the fourth dimension of contemplation. As the fourth dimension embraces the other three dimensions, so Turiya, or primal awareness, embraces the three states of waking, dream, and dreamless sleep. We will try to elucidate in contemporary terms the ancient Vedantic analysis of the three states and Turiya, thus grounding our contemplative experiment in a philosophical understanding of consciousness.

Waking consciousness is the source of the rational, ethical, organizational, technological aspects of human thinking and activity. Turiya does not cancel the waking state but is expressed through it. Thus, waking consciousness, with its precise and practical requirements and responsibilities, is not to be considered as a lower stage that we will eventually transcend through the process of Enlightenment. This waking dimension is to be cherished, to be refined and developed, and finally to be recognized as a perfect expression of Turiya, or Ultimate Consciousness.

In the waking state, there exists the root desire to possess, which dramatizes the sense of separation there. Dream consciousness, which is the source of the romantic, artistic, liturgical, playful aspects of human thinking and activity, centers around the root desire to be possessed, dramatizing the disappearance of separation in the dream state. The state of dreamless sleep is the source of human longing for freedom from limits, the longing to merge in Divine Transcendence or to experience release in various other ways. Yet dreamless sleep involves the root desire to withdraw from thinking and activity. When these three root desires—to possess, to be possessed, and to withdraw—are uprooted by awakening to Turiya, the three basic states of consciousness are not canceled or obliterated but are lived as radiant expressions of primal awareness.

Turiya, or primal awareness, expresses itself as waking, dream, and dreamless sleep, but is neither contained within these states nor definable through them. Turiya is not the rational, ethical, organizational, technological context of waking consciousness. Turiya is not the romantic, artistic, liturgical, playful context of dream that ingresses into waking consciousness. Nor is Turiya the absence of activity and the total release from concern provided by the context of dreamless sleep. Yet these three contexts of consciousness do not and cannot exist apart from Turiya.

Various pictures of Turiya have been suggested, but its nature is essentially unpicturable. Traditional Vedanta philosophy often describes Turiya as *the witness of the three states*. This formulation is not completely adequate, because it suggests a duality between Turiya and the three states witnessed. Modern Vedanta thinkers liken Turiya to a screen, and the three states of consciousness, or all phenomena, are regarded as film projections on the screen. This image is also incomplete, because Turiya is not, like the screen, inert, static, substantial, or objectifiable. Nor is Turiya intrinsically separate from phenomena, as the screen is from the film projections. My Vedanta teacher, Swami Nikhilananda, used to say that Turiya *pervades all the phenomena of the universe as the desert pervades the mirage, but the mirage does not soak a single grain of sand*. This analogy deserves careful and repeated consideration. The phenomena of the universe are themselves only Turiya, just as the drops of mirage water are themselves only sand. There is nothing intrinsically separate from Turiya which can be isolated as the mirage of phenomena. The mirage is simply the desert appearing under certain conditions. Similarly, the mirage of waking, dream, and dreamless sleep is simply Turiya, or primal awareness, experienced through certain conditions. Yet we cannot assert that Turiya is actually touched by the phenomenal realm, for this would be as absurd as to imagine that the mirage actually soaks the desert sand.

Just as Turiya is not a state of consciousness but expresses itself through all states of consciousness, so Turiya is not an experience. From our perspective as seekers, we may imagine that we will someday turn a certain spiritual corner finally to experience the vast new vision of what is truly ultimate. But this is to misunderstand the Ultimate. Turiya is not any particular experience but is what constitutes all experiences. Turiya does not provide new data or even new perspective. Turiya is the primal awareness from which each of our heavenly or earthly experiences is composed.

The principle of a mathematical series is not a member of that series. If we contemplate the series 2, 4, 6, 8, 10, 12, it will dawn on us that there is a principle by which we could generate the series indefinitely. This is how the understanding of Turiya dawns. Turiya is not another number, another experience, another phenomenon. Turiya is the principle of the series. And we have always been aware of Turiya. A small child chants, *Two, four, six, eight, pick up sticks and lay them straight.* When the child comes to understand the principle of this series and is able to generate even integers indefinitely, nothing has actually changed from its early intuitive familiarity with *two, four, six, eight.* This is why Zen masters often make disparaging remarks about supposed Enlightenment experiences. When we proclaim our Enlightenment, they suggest that we are involved in *nonsense* or that we *stink of Zen,* for, glimpsing the principle of the series, we may falsely imagine that we have suddenly experienced Turiya. Actually, we have always intuitively recognized the principle of the series, which is simply primal awareness.

Vivekananda once told his teacher, Ramakrishna, that his highest spiritual aspiration was to remain immersed for days on end in *nirvikalpa samadhi,* the disappearance of all forms into absolute Godhead. He sincerely longed for what he then considered to be the ultimate spiritual experience. But Ramakrishna, who had once spent six months in unbroken nirvikalpa, his body kept alive only by force feeding, replied, *You are a fool. There is a realization higher than nirvikalpa samadhi.* Vivekananda was at that time dedicated to what we have called the third dimension of contemplation, and Ramakrishna was attempting to turn him toward the fourth dimension, or Turiya.

Vivekananda ultimately came to live continuously in the natural realization of Turiya, which Ramakrishna had told him was higher, or more comprehensive, than nirvikalpa samadhi. Occasionally Vivekananda expressed to those around him his understanding of Turiya, which is also called Brahman. His biographer, Nikhilananda, writes: *We see Swami Vivekananda one day seated on a canvas cot under the mango tree in the courtyard of the monastery. Monks and novices about him were busy doing their daily duties. One was sweeping the courtyard with a big broom. Swami Premananda, after his bath, was climbing the steps to the shrine. Suddenly Swami Vivekananda said to a disciple, "Where will you go to seek Brahman? Here, here is the visible Brahman! Shame on those who, neglecting the visible Brahman, set their minds on other things. Can't you see? Here, here, here is Brahman!" These words struck those around him with a kind of electric shock. The broom in the hands of the sweeper stopped. Everyone experienced an indescribable peace. At last the Swami said to Premananda, "Now go to worship."* All structures of work and worship remain after the understanding of Turiya dawns, but they are now experienced with what may be called *indescribable peace*, though this should not suggest a quality sharply divorced from the simple flow of awareness.

Although Turiya is ultimate, it remains immediately accessible. We need not be Enlightened sages such as Vivekananda in order consciously to live Turiya. The initial awakening to Turiya can occur instantaneously for anyone. It does not require long years of meditation. As Ramana Maharshi observed, we do not need a mirror to know that we exist. There is an irreducible quality of immediacy to our conscious being, and that immediacy is Turiya, or primal awareness. Turiya does not obscure any of the structures of consciousness and is not obscured by phenomena. The whole range of ethical responsibility, social action, scientific investigation, and artistic creation, as well as all forms of meditation and worship, remain operative and significant after awakening to Turiya but are engaged in, as Suzuki Roshi suggests, with no *gaining idea*.

In Turiya there is no gain and no loss. Primal awareness is not going anywhere, yet neither is it standing still. Turiya is not a static state, empty of life-forms, which is an image drawn from dreamless sleep. Turiya is the *Is* that intensely and livingly *is,* in and through all that *is,* on all planes and beyond all planes. The *Is* is the principle of the series. Through dealing with members of the series all our lives—*this is, that is, she is, he is*—we realize naturally that there is a principle by which, each moment, countless members of this series are generated but which is not itself a member of the series. This ultimate principle, therefore, is not *something that is.* There is nothing we can conceptually or experientially grasp in order to assert, *This is Is;* yet, nothing is as pervasive or permanent as the *Is.* There is no sublime spiritual experience we can cultivate in order to encounter the *Is,* which is already the core of all experiences, mundane and sublime. Thus there can be no *gaining idea* in Turiya.

Unillumined life in the three states is undertaken through the *gaining idea:* dreamless sleep is the desire to gain release from concern and activity, dreaming is wish-fulfillment, the waking state is fueled by the desire to possess. The *gaining idea* pervades all three states of consciousness when they are not undertaken with the understanding of Turiya, but when the understanding of Turiya awakens, one can immediately begin to undertake the three states without the idea of gain. Least of all can one *gain* Turiya. It is completely inappropriate to desire Turiya or to make efforts to bring Turiya into view. Neither by rejecting nor by courting any experience can we draw closer to Turiya.

Suzuki Roshi indicates how the *gaining idea* can invade contemplative practice, which then subtly confirms our false sense of separateness from Turiya, or primal awareness: *Usually when you practice Zazen you become very idealistic and you set up an ideal or a goal which you strive to attain and fulfill. But as I have often said, this is absurd. When you are idealistic, you have some gaining idea in yourself. By the time you attain your ideal or your goal, your gaining idea will create another ideal . . . you will always be sacrificing yourself now for some ideal in the future. You end up with nothing.* This contemporary Zen master also suggests that the experience of contemplative bliss, even when unsought, can create subtle imaginary barriers to the understanding of Turiya. *Another mistake would be to practice for the sake of the joy you find in it. . . . The best way to do it is without any joy in it, not even spiritual joy . . . forgetting all about yourself in your practice.* Turiya is not an experience of *gaining* bliss or joy. Those who heard Vivekananda invoke the visible Brahman, or Turiya, were spiritually awakened and, as a result, experienced a certain bliss. But their bliss was the removal of all striving to *gain* bliss. Their peace was an absence of any need to *gain* peace. To be free, even for a moment, from the *gaining idea* is blissful and peaceful in this ultimate sense. Yet one cannot forcibly suppress the *gaining idea* in order to *gain* freedom from it. The idea of *gaining* has to dissolve naturally in the completeness and simplicity of Turiya.

Swami Nikhilananda used to say that the Enlightened person *regards every experience as Turiya*, reminding us that we must carefully avoid creating any duality between the three states and Turiya. But the understanding of Turiya turns our ordinary experience of the three states inside out which accounts for the illusory initial sensation that Enlightenment is a revolution in daily consciousness. When we turn a right-handed glove inside out, it becomes a left-handed glove, although we do not change any components of the right-handed glove in the process. Similarly, we do not change the three states of relative consciousness when we realize that they are Turiya, yet our orientation is utterly different. For the Enlightened person, there exist no independent states of consciousness with Turiya somehow pervading them. There is *only* Turiya. The three states, upon closer observation, are revealed as one continuum of Consciousness, one spectrum in which the clear light of Turiya is refracted into three primary colors. With these we color our world.

Mahayana Buddhist scriptures often picture the world as the moon's reflection in water. We reach into the water but can never grasp the reflected moon. However, we can clearly perceive this moon and measure seasons by it. Thus objects and concepts, although they are simply Turiya and therefore as ungraspable as the reflected moon, are nonetheless meaningful. Some objects and concepts can be relied upon for practical purposes, while others can be shown to be imaginary or false. The phenomena of the waking state we call the universe and the discriminations we make among them are not to be dismissed. Phenomena are simply not *there* the way we conventionally imagine them to be. A small child may imagine that an actual moon is floating in the pond. Like that child, we imagine there to be an actual object or concept floating in the pond of our perceiving or thinking, whereas there is only the radiant water of primal awareness, or Turiya.

Far from being inexpressible, Turiya is inevitably expressed by all languages and images. The language of horse racing, for instance, expresses Turiya no less than the sophisticated philosophical languages of Vedanta or Mahayana. While some languages are more conscious than others concerning their grounding in primal awareness, none are more grounded than others. We are tempted to assert this, but such differentiation exists only from the relative standpoint and represents yet another attempt to grasp the reflected moon. Racing horses is as expressive of Turiya as sitting in meditation. A rose is not more *evolved* than an apple blossom. They both grow from the same soil according to the same fundamental principle, although they appear rather different. Similarly, the sage is not more *evolved* than the ordinary person. They both grow from the soil of Turiya. This is why sages so often insist that they are no more special than anyone else.

Turiya, or primal awareness, does not evolve. There is no denying the process of evolution in the phenomenal realm. Yet fundamentally, nothing evolves, because the essential nature of all beings and phenomena is already the radiance of Ultimate Consciousness, or Turiya. Seekers often used to complain to Ramana Maharshi, *My ordinary self is so limited.*

I long to experience the ultimate Self. And Ramana would respond with a question: *Are there really two selves? Is Consciousness two?* Ordinary consciousness is not intrinsically other
than Ultimate Consciousness, or Turiya. The ordinary *is* is
the Ultimate *Is.* One *Is* is all there is. However, such an
affirmation is difficult to assimilate without the intense inspiration provided by the Enlightened person, the Vivekananda or the Ramana Maharshi, who utters it.

Furthermore, if we have not lived and cherished the three
states of consciousness completely, we cannot appreciate the
overwhelming poignance and power of the Enlightened affirmation that all states of consciousness are already Turiya,
or Ultimate Consciousness. We must first live through or
explore intuitively all possible experiences or states of consciousness. The Mahayana and Vedanta philosophies term
our wandering through the infinite varieties of experience
beginingless maya. This vast mirage of experience has been
appearing eternally, and therefore in this present lifetime we
have already experienced every experience if we can identify
with the consciousness of all sentient beings rather than separate ourselves out as limited individuals. Thus the understanding of Turiya is always accessible here and now, even
though the dawning of this understanding presupposes that
one has exhausted or fulfilled all possible experience.

We have thus lived through all experience and would be
consciously Enlightened were we not continually repressing
our own intrinsic Enlightenment. The child learning to swim,
involuntarily represses the sense of its own buoyancy. Awakening to Turiya is learning how to swim, how to give play
to our own buoyancy without disturbing it by frantic efforts
to stay afloat. We must learn to float in primal awareness,
perfectly content, neither rejecting experience nor courting
experience.

Forever, Consciousness has been appearing to travel through
the states of waking, dream, and dreamless sleep, not only
across this planet but on planets in other galaxies, as civilizations that are now flourishing and others that disappeared

ages ago. These are all essentially our own experiences. Zen master Bassui writes: *The layman Ho asked Baso, "What is it that transcends all things in the universe?" Baso answered, "I will tell you after you have swallowed all the water of the West River in one gulp." Upon hearing this, Ho became deeply Enlightened.* The Zen master continues, *How do you swallow all the water of the West River in one gulp? If you grasp the spirit of this, you will be able to go through ten thousand koan at one time and perceive that walking on water is like walking on ground and walking on ground is like walking on water.* Perhaps to swallow the water of the entire West River is to know all the experiences of infinite past, present and future civilizations, in galaxy after galaxy, to be our own intimate experience, our own primal awareness. We are swallowing it all in one gulp. How can we be thirsty anymore?

The four dimensions of contemplation, and their connection with the three states and Turiya, were first suggested to me through a vivid meditation experience that occurred early in my practice and recurred in a more complete form some five years later. It is appropriate to return from our philosophical meditation on Turiya to the spontaneous imagery of spiritual experience on which it rests. Without some grounding in personal experience, contemplative truths can be spoken and yet not understood.

My particular practice involved visualizing Ultimate Reality in the radiant form of an Enlightened sage seated in meditation. I was instructed to begin the visualization by imagining a flame in my heart, and was told that my ishtadeva, a divinely illumined human being, should be imagined sitting within this flame. Thus contemplation begins through an effort of imagination. After some months of this practice, the transformation occurred in which the effort at imagination is superseded, at least temporarily, by the revelatory power of the ishtadeva itself. While attempting to visualize a flame against blackness, suddenly a golden light actually appeared, quite independent of my efforts at concentration. The light was not a flame, but a flame-shaped door to a flame-colored realm. The blackness was simply a wall between dimensions. Spontaneously I approached this open door and perceived within the golden realm my ishtadeva, whose body was the same color as the surrounding light. Moving across the threshold, my own body also appeared as golden radiance. Turning, I noticed a small black flame, the door through which I had entered. I sat before the ishtadeva, or guiding Divinity, feeling intense reverence that gradually became warm intimacy. Then I noticed in the heart of the ishtadeva a white flame, and sensed immediately that this was another door. Moving across this second threshold, into a realm of brilliant white, I discovered the ishtadeva seated there as well. The body of the Enlightened being and my own were bright as snow in sunlight. There was no more personal relationship, but a sense of union. Our two images seemed almost to blend with the white radiance, which was vast rather than intimate. I intuitively looked to the heart of the ishtadeva and perceived there a colorless or transparent flame door. Moving across this threshold into a transparent realm, no forms appeared. There was nothing but pure transparency and the universal awareness that witnessed this transparency.

When the contemplative mood gradually came to an end. I was left with an inner assurance that higher or more comprehensive spiritual dimensions exist and can be experienced. Although this dramatic vision did not recur, my contemplative practice was subtly transformed from active imagination to the quiet receptivity that awaits revelation.

Five years later, on a Tuesday evening, I sat alone with my teacher, Swami Nikhilananda, in his study. The fourth dimension of contemplation, or Turiya, opened unexpectedly. I had not consciously recalled the original experience for years. Spontaneously there returned to me in all vividness the golden realm, then the white realm, and then the transparent realm. The understanding dawned that this transparent realm must also contain a door. No visual metaphor could represent a door in pure transparency, but I knew it was there. Moving across this final threshold, the transcendental witness disappeared as my personal identity had previously disappeared upon entering the transparent realm. Suddenly the three realms—golden, white, and transparent—appeared simultaneously, without obstruction, emerging from one another and disappearing into one another. All realms were the same realmlessness. Even the daily world appeared without any incongruity, sharing this fourth dimension of contemplation: there sat Swami Nikhilananda in his armchair, smoking an Indian cigarette and quietly reading the New York *Times*. There is only Turiya.

BIBLIOGRAPHICAL NOTES

There would be no room for a properly annotated list of writings I have used as background. That would be a book in itself. But I can make a few suggestions for reading in the immediate context of each essay.

Chapter I: Heidegger and Krishnamurti
Heidegger went through two phases in his philosophical development. The major work from his existential period, *Being and Time,* is worth reading for someone who has a strong philosophical bent. It prepares our intellectual understanding for the transition to contemplation. From his second, or contemplative, period, several short works are available in English translation. The work we discussed appears in *Discourse on Thinking,* published by Harper & Row.

Several volumes of Krishnamurti's conversations are available in paperback. The dialogues we discussed appear in *Commentaries on Living, Third Series,* available in paperback from the Theosophical Publishing House.

Chapter II: Ramakrishna
A catalogue listing books in English about Ramakrishna and the illumined souls who surrounded him is available through the Vedanta Press, 1946 Vedanta Place, Los Angeles, California 90028. The quotations in the essay are from the Introduction, by my teacher, Swami Nikhilananda, to his translation of the *Gospel of Ramakrishna,* a thousand-page work published by the Ramakrishna-Vivekananda Center of New

York City, recording vividly and accurately the daily life and teachings of this remarkable being.

Chapter III: Ramana Maharshi

Extensive documentation of the life and teachings of Ramana Maharshi is available in English from Ramanashram, Tiruvannamalai, South India. Some of the quotations of Ramana in the essay are from the excellent biography *Ramana Maharshi and the Path of Self Knowledge,* by his close Western disciple Arthur Osborne, available from Samuel Weiser, Inc. There is also available at the Columbia University library my master's essay, *Ramana Maharshi, Contemporary Life-expression of the Nondualistic Strand of Indian Spirituality,* which is suggestive and contains a useful bibliography.

Chapter IV: Zen Ox-herding

The truly remarkable documents on which this essay is based, the letters of Yaeko to Harada Roshi, appear in the excellent paperback from Doubleday *The Three Pillars of Zen,* edited by Philip Kapleau, which contains invaluable instructions for anyone who wishes to attempt Zen meditation.

Beautiful talks on Zen by the late Suzuki Roshi, founder of the Zen Center in San Francisco, are available in a Weatherhill paperback, *Zen Mind, Beginner's Mind,* from which I quote in the tenth chapter of this book.

The illustrations in this essay were drawn by Eugene Gregan, an American Taoist who creates dresses, jewelry, paintings, and gardens at Look Out Farm, Napanoch, New York.

Chapter V: Plotinus

The quotations in this chapter are from the translation of the complete works of Plotinus, by A. H. Armstrong, in the Loeb Classical Library Series, published by Harvard University Press. A less clear but highly inspired translation of the discourses of Plotinus, by Stephen MacKenna, is published by Pantheon. The *Enneads* of Plotinus are difficult reading, but as they and related writings of the Neoplatonic lineage are discovered among growing numbers of seekers today, a renaissance of the illumined intellect will be sparked. Plotinus is a figure fully comparable in philosophical and spiritual stature to Nagarjuna or Shankara, and he belongs to the Western tradition.

Chapter VI: Hasidic Way
This essay was originally a lecture on the wonderfully warm and suggestive book, which everyone should read, *Souls on Fire*, written by Elie Wiesel, published by Random House and available in paperback. A more philosophical and historical study of Jewish mysticism, which includes the Kabbalah as well as various Hasidic and Messianic movements, is *Major Trends in Jewish Mysticism*, by Gershom Scholem, a Schocken paperback.

Chapter VII: Saint Paul
The translation of Paul's letters quoted in this essay is largely that of the Jerusalem Bible. Everyone should read or reread these letters, ignoring whatever appear as Paul's cultural and personal limitations and meditating on the radical nature of his universal spiritual teaching.

The mystical nature of the Christian practice of Holy Communion, which is not touched by this essay, is very profoundly expressed in *The Eucharist* by Alexander Schmemann, published by St. Vladimir's Seminary Press, Crestwood, New York. Their catalogue of Eastern Orthodox Christian writings is most rewarding.

Chapter VIII: Bawa Muhaiyaddeen
An extensive selection of audio tapes, video tapes, and books of Bawa's spiritual discourses are available from the Bawa Muhaiyaddeen Fellowship, 5820 Overbrook Avenue, Philadelphia, Pennsylvania 19131. The quotations in this chapter are from a personal letter Bawa wrote me from Sri Lanka.

For further elucidation of Islamic Sufism, the writings and

tapes of Sheikh Muzaffer Ozak are highly recommended, available through the Masjid al Farrah, 245 W. Broadway, New York, NY 10013. For the roots of Sufism in the Holy Koran, see *The Heart of the Koran* by Lex Hixon, from the Theosophical Publishing House, Wheaton, Illinois.

Chapter IX: I Ching
The Bollingen edition of the *I Ching*, published by Princeton University Press, is an indispensable book. It contains extensive instructions on how to consult the oracle and rich translations from the ancient commentarial tradition in a style that is more spiritually suggestive than scholarly. In these sixty-four hexagrams, ten thousand books are contained.

Chapter X: Advaita Vedanta
The nondualistic philosophy of Hindu Advaita Vedanta and the Mahayana Buddhist schools of Madhyamika and Yogachara are sister traditions, as I attempted to demonstrate in my doctoral dissertation at Columbia University, *Mahayana Buddhist Influence on the Gauda School of Advaya Vedanta*. This thesis is too technical for the nonspecialist, but the ancient text on which I wrote, the *Gaudapadakarika on the Mandukya Upanisad*, is available in clear English translation with extensive commentary by Swami Nikhilananda. This book, listed along with many other valuable works on Vedanta in the catalogue of the Vedanta Press, noted in this bibliography under Chapter II, is not easy reading but will reward anyone whose contemplative life has an intellectual dimension and who is drawn to the radically nondual teaching of Turiya. Concerning the philosophical expression of Mahayana Buddhist nondualism, I recommend *The Central Philosophy of Buddhism*, by T. R. V. Murti, published by George Allen & Unwin, as well as the writings of various scholars on Zen and Tibetan Tantric Buddhism.

The philosophy and practice of the nondual way is transmitted authentically in the West through various Hindu swamis, Tibetan Buddhist lamas, and Zen Buddhist roshis, some of whom are themselves Westerners. Yet I refrain from mentioning specific teachers or centers, because I am acquainted with so many that such a list would need to be a book in itself. Association with advanced spiritual practitioners and the daily practice of contemplation are the two most potent forces for spiritual growth. Yet the drama of finding an authentic spiritual guide and a contemplative practice that harmonizes with one's particular temperament is often long and complicated, particularly in the spiritually pluralistic climate of today.

Copyright Acknowledgments

Lex Hixon studied philosophy and religion at Yale University, the Graduate Faculties of the New School for Social Research, Union Theological Seminary, and Columbia University, where he received his doctorate degree in comparative religion in 1976. For twenty-two years he has practiced meditation under the guidance of swamis Nikhilananda, Prabhavananda, and Aseshananda of the Ramakrishna Order. From 1970 to 1984 Lex Hixon produced and moderated "In the Spirit," a weekly two-hour radio documentary over WBAI-FM in New York, interviewing numerous spiritual teachers and seekers ranging from Alan Watts to Mother Theresa of Calcutta, from Rabbi Shlomo Carlebach to Swami Satchidananda, and Trungpa Rimpoche, and from Ram Dass and Stephen Gaskin to David Dellinger, Daniel Berrigan, and the Western Zen master and social activist Bernie Glassman.

Receiving the formal transmission of Sheikh Muzaffer-al-Jerrahi of Istanbul and completing the Hajj to Mecca and Medina in 1980, Lex Hixon, in the role of Nur-al-Jerrahi, is a spiritual guide for two Sufi communities in New York and Mexico City. Through the inspiration of Father Alexander Schmemann, Lex Hixon and his wife, Sheila, entered the Eastern Orthodox Church and studied for three years at St. Vladimir's Seminary in Crestwood, New York. They also practice meditation together under the guidance of Lama Tomo Geshe Rimpoche from the Gelugpa Order of Tibetan Buddhism. Under the auspices of the Sarada, Ramakrishna Vivekananda Association, Lex Hixon guides a Vedanta Study Circle in New York. His most recent book, *The Heart of the Koran*, was published in 1988 by the Theosophical Society Press in Wheaton, Illinois.